HOW to TOILET-TRAIN YOUR CAT

21 DAYS TO A LITTER-FREE HOME

BY PAUL KUNKEL

HOW TO TOILET-TRAIN YOUR CAT

21 DAYS TO A LITTER-FREE HOME

BY PAUL KUNKEL

Illustrations by
Kimble Pendleton Mead

Workman Publishing • New York

No well-published book is a solitary effort. Therefore, I wish to thank everyone at Workman Publishing, especially Peter Workman for his insight, Sally Kovalchick for her encouragement and Shawna McCarthy for her careful editing. Thanks also to Brian Kilcommons, Beverly Moore and Brian Coates, Barnum and Bailey, Douglas Weiss, Ronald and Rose Morin, Mary Miliser, Lee Frank, Michael Cader, Mao-Zelda and, of course, Chee.

Copyright © 1991 by Paul Kunkel

Library of Congress Cataloging-in-Publication Data

Kunkel, Paul.
How to toilet train your cat: 21 days to a litter-free cat / Paul Kunkel.
   p.   cm.
Includes bibliographical references.
ISBN 0-89480-828-1 : $5.95
1. Cats — Toilet training.   I. Title.
SF446.6.K86   1991
636.8'088'7 — dc20   90-50948
                                       CIP

Cover design by Paul Hanson
Cover photo by Alice Su
Book design by Tom Starace
Book illustrations by Kimble Pendleton Mead

Workman Publishing Company, Inc.
708 Broadway
New York, New York 10003

Manufactured in the United States of America
First printing April 1991

10 9 8 7 6 5 4 3 2 1

CONTENTS

INTRODUCTION

As any cat owner will tell you, the bond between cats and humans is as strong as it is enduring. Both affectionate and independent, a cat can be dignified and inscrutable one moment, playful and loving the next. Pressing himself* against your leg, looking up with a fiery gleam in his eye, his intoxicating purr and soft furry warmth working their eternal magic—these are pleasures only a cat lover can know.

MAN'S BEST FRIEND?

What began as a quiet love affair in Egypt more than six thousand years ago has blossomed into something of a mass movement. In 1980 a national cat census conducted by the American Pet Food Institute found that thirty-five million cats were living in American households, while there were fifty-two million dogs. Today, however, the cat outnumbers man's best friend by a considerable margin—sixty million, compared to only fifty-five million dogs—with its popularity showing no signs of slowing. This means that more than thirty million American households own, or are owned by, one or more cats.

*For ease of language, I've decided to refer to cats as "him" in this text. You can, of course, toilet train female cats with equal success.

What explains this sudden switch? An increase in one- and two-person households; the growing number of two-paycheck families; the increasing number of apartment dwellers; and a desire among young couples and older people to take on "low-maintenance" pets.

According to Phyllis Wright, vice president of the Humane Society of the United States, "cats are the genetically engineered pet for the 1990s. They are much less demanding than dogs and much more conducive to a busy lifestyle than any other pet."

PROBLEMS, PROBLEMS

Yet this very popularity has fostered the myth that cats, unlike dogs with their many obedience and behavior problems, can essentially do no wrong. With this misconception in mind, the uninitiated will bring home their first kitten in total ignorance, only to grow disenchanted as the adorable kitten matures into a somewhat less cute adult. Slotted into the daily household routine, the cat's day rapidly shrinks into a dull round of trips to the kitchen for food and water and to the litter box to excrete same — over and over, day after day, week after week. Eventually, as the owner's interest wanes, the daily ritual of cleaning the litter box becomes an every-other-day chore, then every third day, until the box becomes such a headache for cat and owner that the cat begins to "just miss" the litter box, or dig so vigorously that he leaves litter scattered everywhere. In both cases, the cat is trying to say something in the only way he knows how. Yet no one listens until the cat avoids the litter box altogether in favor of a more absorbent material: your mother's Persian rug, the back of your closet, or that quiet spot behind the couch that only a cat can reach.

According to Dr. Dale Olm, chief animal behavior specialist at the New York office of the American Society for the Prevention of Cruelty to Animals, soiling problems cause more cats to be abandoned or put to sleep than any other single issue. "The problem is huge," says Dr. Olm. "Slowly the smell becomes so bad that no one wants to visit you anymore. Finally it becomes so bad that even the cat revolts and owners get rid of the cat because of its 'abnormal' behavior." Yet the truth of the matter, says Dr. Olm, is that "there is no such thing as 'abnormal' behavior in cats, only 'normal' behavior in an abnormal situation."

KITTENS MUST BE TRAINED

As faithful pets, cats rely on us not only for their food and water, health and well-being, they depend on us to provide the conditions they need to become good companions in our homes. Like young children, kittens and cats must be trained to prevent their natural predelictions, developed over millions of years of evolution, from developing into unacceptable behavior. Yet they can't train themselves, so they need our help. "A misbehaving cat is nearly always the fault of the owner," says Dr. Olm, "not the cat." But, before we can help them, we must first understand them.

Even though mother cats teach their kittens to bury their wastes as soon as they are able to dig loose dirt, it is both unnatural and unhealthy for an adult cat to bury his wastes in the same spot every day. Why? According to Dr. Olm, "Cats are both attracted to and repelled by the smell of their own wastes. On the one hand, they habitually go to the litter box, because it's where they've always gone. Yet one of the cat's most basic instincts is to equate the smell of its own waste products with danger." This is because cats in the wild use their highly fragrant urine and feces to ward off potential predators and rivals, as well as to mark

the boundaries of their territory. Therefore a cat will rarely do his business in the same spot twice, preferring instead to spread his droppings in a large ring that encircles his nest. Near the nest, where the smell of this "scent barrier" is nonexistent, the cat feels perfectly safe. Yet toward the edge of his territory, where the smell of accumulated droppings becomes quite noticeable, the cat must be on his guard at all times.

Not surprisingly, cats using a single litter box often develop a form of territorial-anxiety behavior that results from enormous stress. Initially, the cat will pace as though he were a caged animal, meowing loudly and clawing everything in sight. As the stress builds, reactions can take many forms, until finally the cat begins to leave his droppings everyplace *but* the litter box.

One way to determine whether your cat has a problem in the making is to place two litter boxes at opposite ends of the home as far apart as possible. If the cat begins to use both boxes right away, particularly if he urinates in one box and defecates in the other, your cat is well on his way to having a problem—even if he has yet to have his first "accident." What can you do?

If you're like most people, you change the cat's litter and clean the litter box every day, slowly turning yourself from a loving owner into an obedient servant who jumps every time the cat goes to his box. Ultimately, instead of enjoying your pet, you can come to look upon him as a furry little loafer who is more trouble than he is worth.

Why allow a cat to turn you into a slave? If we agree to let the cat live with us—giving him the run of the house, feeding him, and caring for him with toys, treats, and regular trips to the veterinarian—it's only fair that the cat live with us on *our* terms. As with people it's only right that your cat should work for his living by behaving in ways that make his owners' lives, as well as his own, a little easier and a lot more enjoyable.

THE 21-DAY TOILET TRAINING PROGRAM

As you will discover in the following pages, it's not only possible to prevent your cat from developing bad litter-box habits, it's easy to prevent bad habits before they develop by teaching your cat to give up his litter box entirely and use the bathroom toilet—a simple, sanitary, odor-free solution that any normal, healthy cat between six months and ten years of age can master—using a method we call the 21-Day Program. If you take the time to toilet train your cat, the temporary inconvenience of training will pay enormous rewards. Not only will your cat be happier and healthier using a toilet instead of a box, he will be a joy to live with for the rest of his days.

But before you can train your cat, you must first train yourself. No matter what kind of cat you own or how old he is, you should take the time to learn what makes your cat tick and how cats develop, as well as how their mothers raise them in the wild. This will go a long way toward understanding your cat's inner nature and will dispel many misconceptions that owners have about their cats. As you will see in chapter 1, cats must *learn* to dig and bury their wastes — as well as most other "catlike" behaviors, such as grooming, prowling, stalking, and hunting — as kittens. Kittens and cats are highly adaptable, capable of imitating any behavior that is within their capabilities. In fact, research has shown that they will learn virtually anything their "mother" teaches them, whether the teacher be their natural mother, another cat, or even a member of another species — such as you.

Before you can toilet train your cat, you must first ensure that he has been thoroughly litter trained. Therefore, in chapter 2 you will find a simple, foolproof method for litter training any cat, whether it be a young kitten or an older cat living indoors for the first time. In chapter 3 you will get a cat's eye view of the litter box, and a glimpse at exactly what is used to make cat litter, with an analysis of the potential health risks associated with a material that most cats ingest nearly every day of their lives. As you might suspect, there are many reasons why no sensible pet owner should ever allow their cat to use chemically treated commercial cat box filler.

Once the foundation has been set, in chapter 4 you will find a simple step-by-step procedure for toilet training any litter-trained cat in approximately 21 days, using nothing more exotic than a litter box, a pile of magazines, a roll of plastic wrap, and a little common sense. If you follow the program closely, paying strict attention to the timing sequence, you will ensure your cat's success. Of course toilet training, like any other skill, takes time to practice.

By following the guidelines offered in this book, you will not only have a well-behaved cat who works for his living, you will have a friend whom you can incorporate into your home and make a real member of your family.

Aside from ridding you of anxiety — that horrible feeling when guests are about to arrive ("Did we clean the litter box today? Did the cat make a mess again?") — and the problem of recurring illness associated with litter boxes, toilet training spares you the trouble and expense of keeping a litter box always underfoot. It pays off in good old dollars and cents you would otherwise spend in buying litter, litter pans, and cleansers, as well as in potential savings in veterinarian's bills since it helps avoid the medical problems that litter boxes can cause.

THE RESULTS: SPECTACULAR

Toilet training also means that your feline friend can take care of himself in your absence — as long as you keep an adequate supply of food and water in the kitchen and the bathroom door open (with the toilet lid up!). He can even go traveling with you, without your having to worry about having a litter box around. After all, toilets are more or less the same wherever you go. Once the cat learns to use your facilities at home, it will be a simple matter to show him where to go when you're away (lifting him up, if necessary, to make sure he knows what you have in mind). As peculiar as it sounds, toilet training works anywhere, as long as the cat is properly trained.

Ultimately a toilet-trained cat is both happier and healthier, with a gleam in his eye and an extra bounce in his step. He's healthier, because the territorial stress associated with the smell of his litter box has been lifted, like a giant cloud of pollution, eliminating the source of many of his most basic behavioral problems. The cat is happier, because you are happier. Instead of being a burden, he's a source of pride and enjoyment that reveals itself every day. And isn't that what it's all about?

1

WHAT IS
A CAT?

According to fossil records, the first cats roamed the earth more than ten million years ago and assumed their present size around six million years ago — *long* before man first made his appearance. Molded by evolution into a solitary nocturnal species with unparalleled hunting skills, the domestic house cat's nearest relative, the African wildcat (*Felis lybica*), still inhabits the plains of north Africa just as he did when Egyptian civilization emerged from the darkness of prehistory more than eight thousand years ago.

ANCIENT ORIGINS

Like all early civilizations, the Egyptians founded their economy on the cultivation of grain. Stored in enormous silos, this grain attracted rodents which (according to the Old Testament) soon reached plague-like concentrations. Lured by such easy pickings, *Felis lybica* entered Egyptian households as mousers *par excellence* and remained there as pets for the next eight thousand years.

Since the Egyptians had no concept of modern genetics, the process of domestication through selective breeding doesn't seem to have occurred during the thousands of years that Egyptians and cats lived together. Indeed, comparing skeletons and early pictures of *Felis lybica* to the modern house cat, they look virtually identical. The first known painting of a domesticated cat appears in the Egyptian tomb of Ti (c. 2,600 B.C.), where a modern-looking orange tabby with a flashy grin is shown wearing an ornamental collar. In another tomb (c. 1,900 B.C.), seventeen cats were laid out next to their deceased owner — carefully mummified and wrapped in linens, each with his own mummified mouse and bowl of preserved milk.

As godly symbols representing the sun god Osiris and the mother god Isis, cats in Egypt were protected to such an extent that anyone encountering a dead feline in the streets of ancient Cairo would flee rather than risk an accusation of murder. According to contemporary accounts, the death of a cat sent entire families into mourning, with the male members shaving their eyebrows as a sign of grief.

So total was the Egyptians' veneration for cats that when the Persian king Cambiase launched his invasion of Egypt in 595 B.C., he assured himself of victory by arming his soldiers with pictures of the holy animal on every sword and shield. Eventually the Persians conquered the whole of Egypt, thus allowing the sacred cats to escape on trading ships to the Middle East and Europe.

The speed with which they spread is indicated by the fact that the word for cat is virtually the same in every European language: Spanish (gato), German (katze), Dutch and Danish (kat), Polish (kot), Swedish and Norwegian (katt), English (cat), French (chat), Maltese (qattus), modern Latin (catus), and Greek (gata), as well as Syrian (quato) and Arabic (quett) — all of them derived from the ancient Latin *cautus* (meaning "astute") and the Indo-European root *ǵhad* (meaning "to catch or grasp"). The most common nickname — "kitty" — stems from the Turkish word for cat (kedi).

A REMARKABLE SPECIMEN

Even after centuries of living under man's care, domestic cats today remain extremely close to their ancestral form. Despite superficial changes of coat color, size, and marking, even the most pampered house cat is but one step from the predatory rat killer that guarded the food stores of ancient Egypt.

Everything about him inspires a sense of awe. With a magnificent hunter's head, a powerful yet sensitive mouth, and the teeth of a true carnivore, the cat has ears that can pick up any sound, eyes capable of seeing in the dimmest light, and a nose that detects anything the cat cannot see or hear. Long, limber, and amazingly flexible, the cat's body is perfectly designed for the silent stalk and the graceful leap, combining strength and agility with remarkable speed. His strong back and leg muscles allow the cat to jump many times his own height, with reflexes that guarantee he always lands on his feet. And his remarkable sense of balance, developed thousands of years ago when cats spent most of their time in the branches of trees, means he can scale any height and walk atop the narrowest fence, using his tail the way a tightrope walker uses his pole.

In addition to his ordinary senses, many owners feel their cats have supernatural powers. Stories of cats becoming alarmed moments before an earthquake suggest that they are capable of detecting things that we cannot. But, according to cat expert Desmond Morris, this "sixth sense" is merely the cat's reaction to minute vibrations and the subtle changes in air pressure that precede such major events.

Because of these and other qualities, cats have been the subject of intense scrutiny in recent years. Trying to unlock the secrets to his behavior, scientists have studied *Felis catus* in every conceivable habitat — from wild sub-arctic islands with densities of less than one cat per square mile to modern industrial cities with more than one thousand cats per square mile — marveling at the animal's stunning flexibility and highly developed hunting and survival skills.

ARE CATS DOMESTICATED ... OR WILD?

Of all the species that have left the wild and chosen to live with us, only cats have retained the skills and equipment necessary to return to the wild. In fact, many "domestic" cat breeds grow larger and heavier in the wild, occasionally reaching the same size as truly wild species. In the jungles of Southeast Asia, for example, wild Siamese cats have been known to grow to nearly twice the size of their housebound siblings, while in the western United States domestic shorthairs the size of bobcats can be found living near suburbs.

But what about house cats that venture out periodically? In a recent study conducted in the village of Felmersham, England, Dr. John H. Lawton, a animal researcher at the University of London, found that house cats occupied the top of the local food chain, being twice as effective at killing small mammals and birds as local foxes and one and one-half times as effective as local barn owls — even though, as well-fed "domestic" animals, they did not need to hunt at all.

This makes the modern cat something of a paradox — a species that is both dependent and independent — preferring to accept our care and affection without giving up his ancient predatory ways. For this reason, scientists aren't sure whether cats are truly domesticated.

While touring villages in southern Egypt in the late nineteenth century, the German explorer George Schweinfurth observed children catching *Felis lybica* kittens and raising them as pets. Schweinfurth himself "procured several of these cats, which, after they had been kept tied up for several days, seemed to lose a considerable measure of their ferocity and adapt themselves to an indoor existence so as to approach in many ways to the habits of the common cat."

Could it be that the cat, like man, simply changes his behavior to fit a new set of circumstances? Has the cat, in other words, domesticated itself?

Whatever the case, all house cats share certain innate characteristics with their wild cousins that reveal themselves from the very beginning of every kitten's life. Being aware of these qualities and the way they develop as kittens grow will make you more aware of what makes your cat tick.

A KITTEN IS BORN ...

Because of the harsh conditions under which their ancestors lived, all mother cats raise their kittens as though they were actually living in the wild. From tiny defenseless kitten to self-sufficient adult, the cat's physical and mental development is extraordinarily fast, many times faster than our own, and always fascinating to watch.

Totally blind and deaf at birth, a furry sausage-shaped blob weighing only three or four ounces, the newborn kitten enters a world in which he must instantly use his highly sensitive nose to find his mother. Once he picks up the scent, he wiggles and squirms, exerting every ounce of his strength to move himself into position, where he makes an instinctive treading motion with his paws to stimulate the mother to produce milk.

The kitten's first fourteen days are roughly equal to a human baby's first nine months. By the fifth day, already twice his original size, though not yet able to see, the kitten's sense of smell is almost fully de-

Pavlov's Cat

Douglas Weiss knew he had a problem when his cat Willow began to leave little presents in the bathroom shower.

"When I realized that she was using the shower drain as her litter box, I began to adjust her routine step-by-step," he recalls. "First, I placed her litter box in the shower, directly over the drain. Then, as soon as Willow began using the litter, I closed off the shower and placed her box next to the toilet." Raising the box was no problem, says Weiss, "but after I removed the litter box and installed the plastic wrap under the toilet seat, it took several weeks for her to use the litter without squeezing into the center of the toilet seat."

Eventually Weiss intervened directly. "First I cut a hole in the center of the wrap and left litter scattered around the hole. Then I picked her up and placed her on the toilet seat. Every time she tried to step onto the litter, I put her feet back onto the seat," says Weiss. "The first time she did it, I made her feel like she had just spoken her first word."

According to Weiss, "the idea of praise produced a Pavlovian response" in Willow. In his most famous study, conducted in the early 1920s, Pavlov installed a red light in a dog's pen and turned it on before every feeding. Eventually, Pavlov's dog became so conditioned by the red light that the dog would begin to salivate when the light was turned on, even though there was no food present. "Praise became such an important part of Willow's toilet training," he concludes, "that she waits until I return from work, then runs to the bathroom, expecting me to follow."

BRIAN COATES

veloped — capable of identifying not only his mother and littermates, but the specific nipple he must return to for feeding. Placed as much as four feet from the nest, a four-day-old kitten will immediately sniff the air to determine the proper direction and struggle for hours, exhausting himself if necessary, in order to return to the comforting smell of the nest.

Such instincts are crucial for the kitten's viability in the first few weeks. But instinct alone is not enough. Once they are secure in the nest, the mother must teach her kittens a number of survival lessons, first among them being the proper disposal of their bodily wastes. In the wild, this is accomplished by carefully cleaning the kittens during the first weeks of life and later showing them how to dig and bury their wastes — a skill that kittens use to avoid predators until they are old enough to leave their mother and fend for themselves.

During the first four weeks of life, the mother spends most of her time protecting her kittens, and at least 40 percent of her time nursing, encouraging the kittens to suckle as much as they can. When she's not feeding, the mother cleans her kittens by licking them from head to tail, stroking each kitten's chest to aid his digestion and his lower belly to stimulate him to eliminate. Until the age of two weeks, no kitten has the physical ability to eliminate on his own. By licking his underbelly, the mother triggers the kitten's urogenital reflex, ingesting the kitten's microscopic wastes as she licks.

Because a kitten can only eliminate when his mother stimulates his urogenital reflex, he is prevented from attracting predators by soiling the nest. This continues for as long as the nest remains the center of activity, until the kittens reach about four weeks of age — by which time they are up and running around.

Then, toward the end of the fourth week, the mother cat in the wild will suddenly move her kittens, dragging them one at a time by the scruff of the neck to a new nest closer to their source of food. This way, the kittens can watch her drag her prey to them, arousing their carnivorous responses at the same time that they begin to eat their first solid food.

In the home, however, a cat may or may not move her kittens. If she does, she will move them to a fresh spot somewhat closer to the kitchen — to bring them closer to her source of food. Even though she has never lived in the wild, and her "prey" is cooked and deposited in a bowl at the same time each day, instinct dictates that she drag it to her young as though it were freshly killed. It will do no good to try to return the kittens to the original nest. Like the act of hunting itself, the ritual of a mother moving kittens and dragging food to them is so ancient that no amount of domestic comfort will cause her to suppress it.

Once the kittens are situated in their new nest,

they learn the details of feline behavior by observing and imitating their mother's every move — the way she holds herself, the way she sits, grooms herself, and above all, the way she stalks and prowls. As a result, the moment she stops grooming her kittens, they begin to groom themselves and play with each other in a more determined fashion, training their hunters' instincts as their tiny bodies continue to grow. The technique of visual recognition, stealth, and the art of the prowl are all learned during this critical time by kittens watching their mother and practicing on each other.

HOW DO KITTENS LEARN TO USE A LITTER BOX?

Eventually, by following their mother and picking up scent clues, the kittens arrive at an area of soft dirt where they learn an extremely valuable lesson. As the kittens observe, the mother cat digs a small hole with her forepaws, positions herself over the hole, relieves herself, and covers it with her forepaws. When she walks away, the kittens then approach the spot, move the particles of dirt with their paws, and record the smell with their sensitive little noses.

Though a mother cat in the wild often leaves her wastes exposed when she is away from the nest, she will always bury them in her kittens' presence to hide

the smell (thus keeping the nest area safe from predators) and to teach the technique to her kittens.
Ordinarily, the kittens will urinate in the same area
right away as a way of imitating their mother (and
will later return to that spot in reaction to the smell).

This apparently sudden response is often described
as "inherent," "innate," or "instinctive" behavior — the
argument being that cats are such fastidious creatures
that they naturally hide and cover their wastes without having to be instructed.

INSTINCTIVE IMITATION

Yet the instinctive element is not the ability to perform the behavior, but the ability to *learn* it. By the
time his eyes open wide enough to see, every kitten
begins to study and imitate the actions of his mother,
his littermates, and any other cat or species that happens to be in the house.

In other words, kittens learn whatever they are
taught. To demonstrate this phenomenon, the Chinese
biologist Zing Yang Kuo studied two groups of kittens:
one group of twenty kittens raised by their mothers
in a mouse-killing household; and another group of
twenty raised with mice. Among the first group,
where each kitten had seen his mother kill a mouse,
eighteen out of twenty managed to kill a mouse on
the first attempt (nine of them eating it as well).

Among the second group, only three kittens out of twenty managed to subdue a mouse but none could actually kill one.

In one of the most extreme examples of this response ever recorded, an orphaned male kitten raised with a litter of puppies *learned to urinate by lifting his leg on a tree after observing his male dog companions doing so.*

This ability to learn through observation alone assures that a cat will learn to bury his waste (in a specific area when in the wild, or in a litter box in the home). Yet *it must first be demonstrated by his mother, another cat, or a member of another species, such as yourself* (see chapter 2).

By the eighth week, kittens in the wild consume less and less of their mother's milk (eating more and more solid food). Then, at the end of the eighth week or the beginning of the ninth, the mother will suddenly deny them access to her nipples and will even chase them away, eventually leaving them to fend for themselves.

FROM KITTEN TO ADULT

For domestic-breed kittens in the wild, the end of the weaning process is an intensely disorienting experience. Left to his own devices, a kitten wanders aimlessly, enduring a profound sense of distress in the first weeks after leaving his mother. Consequently he soon loses his juvenile charm, finds his own territory, and defends it by using his urine and feces as territorial markers, eventually developing into a solitary hunter with many of the same behaviors as true wild cats.

Yet most kittens never experience the wild. Leaving their mother one day, they often take up residence with a new, human family the next. As a result, "many of the kitten's juvenile habits are preserved long beyond the normal time," says the noted animal researcher Paul Leyhausen.

Tamed by the sequence of their upbringing, switching immediately from littermates to humans, most kittens become attached to both species and consider themselves members of both. The moment a human assumes responsibility for feeding and caring for a cat, says Leyhausen, "the cat will continue in a state of juvenile dependency, viewing the human as a stand-in for its mother."

This "kittenish" behavior is familiar to anyone who has felt the characteristic "kneading" motion that a cat makes while sitting in one's lap. This motion is identical to the grip a newborn kitten uses to attach himself to his mother while nursing. The fact that cats often follow their owners is another sign of kittenish dependence. Even the fact that a cat will purr when stroked by a human — the same way he did with his mother — suggests that adult cats view their owners as stand-ins for their mothers.

TAME ON THE OUTSIDE, WILD AT HEART

That furry bundle purring away in your lap can quickly become an effective hunter, however, given the proper stimulus. Spotting a squirrel or chipmunk, he quietly switches from kitten to killer. Suddenly, he becomes very still, crouches, flexes his muscles, and twitches his rear, prepared to launch an attack. Then, out of the corner of his eye, he spots you and, after a brief moment of indecision, turns about and offers a "Who me?" expression, as though hunting were the farthest thing from his mind.

This "split personality," the ability of a domestic cat to lead a double life, as a kitten on the outside and an occasional hunter within, is the key difference between domestic cats and their wild cousins. The more a domestic kitten is handled by humans early in life, the more "kittenlike" he will become as an adult. Yet that in no way changes the cat's inner nature — that spark of wildness that still links him with his

African ancestors even after thousands of years of domestic life.

All we can do as owners is try to understand our cat's "wild" side and make allowances for what cannot be changed.

THE NEED FOR TERRITORY

Chief among the cat's "wild" instincts is the need to establish and guard his own turf. Developed millions of years before the first Egyptian ever laid eyes on a cat, territorial behavior is central to the cat's identity, second only to self-preservation as the strongest of all feline behaviors.

Generally speaking, territory is that collection of sights, sounds, and, above all, smells that a cat considers an extension of himself. Cats define their territory in terms of the *nest*, where the cat eats and sleeps, and a larger, more loosely defined, area around the nest called the *home range*.

For a cat in the wild, the home range might be a small forest, the sunny side of a mountain, or an entire valley with space for hunting areas, rest spots, escape routes, and private watering holes. For a free-ranging domestic cat living on a farm, the home range might include twenty acres around the farmhouse. In the suburbs, a cat might claim the house as his nest and the backyard (plus two or three adjoining backyards) as his home range. Yet in the city, where space is tight, the nest might be only one or two rooms, with the home range limited to the tiny enclosed space behind a townhouse, a balcony, or a spare room. Yet no matter how much (or how little) space a cat can claim, all cats exercise the same territorial instinct and will do everything in their power to claim a certain area as their own — using the most highly developed of all their faculties — their sense of smell.

THE IMPORTANCE OF SCENT

It's difficult to overestimate the sensitivity of a cat's nose. Much more discriminating than our own, cats can identify smells that few other species can even detect. The secret is an intricate nasal membrane folded so that its surface area is many times greater than that in most animals of a comparable size. The average cat's nose has nineteen million nerve endings as opposed to the average human's five million.

What's more, cats also have a second olfactory system known as Jacob's organ, an unbelievably sensitive vomeronasal instrument located at the back of the throat.

When he wants to do some serious sniffing, the cat will first inhale through his nose, then stretch his neck and appear to grimace, panting slightly as he draws air through his mouth across Jacob's organ. Using his

The Cat Who Trained Himself

Eighteen years ago, Mary Miliser's son found Fred shivering inside an old box, all alone on the outskirts of Chicago.

Eventually, Mary moved to Sequim, Washington, whereupon Fred became an outdoor cat. "The house has a cat door that allows him to go in and out," says Mary, "so rather than use his litter box, Fred preferred to go outside."

Twice a year, however, constant rains kept Fred indoors. "Sometimes he would have to stay in for days at a time — yet he never seemed to use his litter box," Mary remembers. Only later, and quite by accident, did she discover why.

"I was standing in the bathroom, when, all of a sudden, I heard the sound of water running." Mary turned around, and there was Fred perched up on the edge of the toilet.

When asked how Fred got the idea to use the toilet instead of his litter box, Mary shrugs. "Maybe he thinks he's human. After all, we use the toilet. Why shouldn't he?"

Once Mary realized that Fred's using the toilet was no fluke, she made certain to keep the bathroom door open and the toilet seat down, particularly on cold or rainy days. "Eventually I emptied out his litter box and put it away," she says. "But I didn't dare tell anyone." That was in 1980. Six years later, the only cat known to have taught himself to use a toilet wandered off and never returned, taking his secrets with him.

· C A S E ·
· S T U D Y ·

nose and throat in combination, a cat can smell nine times more than the average human, including the scent of another cat left days, or even weeks, before.

For this reason, most cats are extremely conscious of smells, both pleasant and unpleasant, and can remember them for a very long time. This highly developed "scent memory" stems from the animal's very first experience — when the tiny, sightless kitten must locate his mother's nipple and identify each of his littermates by scent alone.

Considering that the cat's nose is so discriminating, the list of substances he responds to is immense. Pleasant scents include items as diverse as yeast, fennel, wet plaster, motorcycle grease, stagnant water, freshly cooked corn, and even old clothes.

But the list of smells that cats can't stand is equally long. One of the most common is nitrogen — the tiniest trace of which comes from canned food the moment it turns bad. This is why so many cats refuse to eat their food the day after it is opened. Another is common household vinegar. With certain exceptions, no cat will go near chemical smells, especially those of cleansers containing pine oil, ammonia, or virtually any disinfectant. One exception is the chlorine scent of fresh laundry — which explains why many cats prefer sleeping in the clothes hamper (or even inside the dryer!). Another is gasoline, which many cats, like people, sniff delightedly.

Suffice it to say that no odor escapes your cat's attention. Yet of all the millions upon millions of substances in the natural world, nothing sets a cat off quite like the smells that cats make themselves: at one of the spectrum is the faint, musky, almost undetectable odor produced by scent glands on a cat's head and face, and at the other is the sharp room-clearing stench of his urine and feces — the same smells that all cats use to mark and maintain their territory.

TERRITORIAL MARKING

In recent years, the most interesting research on domestic cats has focused on their intense territorial behavior and the importance of scent to a cat's well-being. Depending on their distance from the nest, all cats mark their territory in four distinct ways.

Allomarking. Allomarking is the most common marking technique, something you've seen your cat do a thousand times. First the cat rubs his mouth on the desired spot, then follows with his forehead, cheek, and the entire length of his body, marking the spot by transferring a scent from tiny sebaceous glands located on his head and the base of his tail to the object in question.

Though completely odorless to humans, the scent left by head rubbing is like Limburger cheese to a cat. Yet such a tiny amount is deposited when a cat rubs, it is difficult to see. Should your cat happen to rub his head against a clean window, look quickly and you will notice a slight smudge that quickly disappears. That's the mark of the scent gland at work.

Given the opportunity, a cat will rub his head and body on the leg of every chair, table, person, the corner of every wall and door — and every other surface within his reach, over and over again. So when he rubs passionately on your new running shoes, he's not praising your choice of footwear, he's telling every other cat in the world that these particular shoes are part of his territory.

As Aesop once observed, "the cat always leaves a mark on his friend," and most cat owners wouldn't have it any other way.

Clawing and Scratching. Cats also claw deep visible scratches into any vertical object they can reach, such as a tree (if the territory is a forest) or the arm of your favorite chair (if the territory is your living room). As you know, cats scratch to exercise their claws, removing the dead outer layer so that a new claw can grow in its place. Yet clawing is also a means of marking territory by spreading the scent produced by tiny glands in the cat's paws onto the object he is scratching. No one knows whether the scent from scratching is stronger or different from the scent from face-rubbing.

Urine Spraying. Surely the most offensive way a male cat can advertise his presence is by forcibly spraying his urine, laden with noxious pheromones, onto any available surface (a tree, a rock, your five-hundred-dollar speaker) as a way of expressing outrage, stress, or sexual desire. It is quite a different urge than the cat's need to void. While urinating, a cat squats in a characteristic fashion, expelling his urine vertically. While spraying, however, the cat stands erect and forces his stinky calling card out horizontally, holding his tail up while wiggling his backside — leaving behind an odor that is so pungent that it lasts for weeks in open country and is positively mind-boggling in an enclosed space. (Fortunately for owners, domestic cats do not exhibit this behavior if they have been neutered before the cat reaches six months of age.)

Urination and Defecation. Though spraying is the strongest social statement a cat can make, cats do not use it to establish or maintain their territory. Instead, they use their urine and feces. Both domestic cats that return to the wild and free-ranging domestics living on farms and in country suburbs follow similar patterns when nature calls. Rather than doing their business in a single spot near the nest, as cats do when they are litter trained, free-ranging cats always

To Drink or Not to Drink

When Lisa Gabbay, a graphic designer, first saw Darth more than five years ago, the tiny black kitten was wandering the streets of Danbury, Connecticut. "He couldn't have been more than six months old," she recalls. "Since I had three cats at the time, I decided to try to toilet train him using the spare bathroom." Thus, keeping the litter box in its normal place, she set up a Kitty Whiz plastic liner over the toilet in the spare bathroom, and filled it with cat litter. Within two weeks, Darth was using the toilet regularly. In time, Darth also began to use the toilet in the other bathroom — as a water bowl.

This situation was perfect until Lisa moved into a small Manhattan apartment with Darth, who took to the toilet right away. "But with only one bathroom in the apartment," she recalls, "he had no place to drink. He refused to relieve himself and drink from the same toilet. Nor would he drink from his blue water bowl, even when I placed it in the bathroom. When I could, I let him drink straight from the faucet. But I couldn't run the water 24 hours a day." Eventually, Darth became dehydrated. "That's when a friend suggested that I exchange his blue water bowl for a white bowl — the same shape and color as the toilet bowl." It worked like a charm.

· C A S E ·
S T U D Y

relieve themselves as far from the nest as possible to avoid detection by predators, taking care never to use the same place twice. Indeed most cats put a considerable distance between one event and the next, often going in a different direction from the nest each time nature calls.

In addition, free-ranging cats are more likely *not* to bury their wastes — precisely the opposite of what most owners consider "normal" feline behavior.

THE SCENT BARRIER

Since he rarely travels beyond the distance of his farthest excretion, the pattern that a cat makes with his urine and feces eventually becomes the boundary within which his territory is defined — an area that can vary from as much as one hundred and seventy acres for an extremely dominant male to as little as five acres for a female tending a litter of kittens.

No matter what size their territory, free-ranging cats exert amazing persistence and energy to scent-mark the perimeter of that territory, with males urinating as much as thirty times per hour and females five or six times per hour. Doing this systematically, day after day, at a more or less fixed distance from the nest, the cat eventually forms a "scent barrier" around the nest designed not only to confuse predators (by placing the cat's scent consistently away from the nest) and to warn rival cats that another cat is present, but to protect the cat himself from straying beyond his own territory.

As a rule, a cat in the wild feels secure only within his own scent barrier. Once he reaches the edge of his territory and detects the smell of his own urine and feces, instinct tells him to turn around and retreat toward the center of his territory — an automatic response that is critical to the cat's long-term survival in the wild. For if a cat should accidentally cross his own scent barrier and attempt to reenter his territory at another point along the scent barrier, the cat would automatically turn away — thus becoming hopelessly lost.

TERRITORIAL STRESS

Domesticated cats living in a home with a large and fragrant litter box often become edgy and nervous, since the same smell in the wild usually means danger. Indeed, the stronger the smell, the more vulnerable a cat feels — as though he were forced to live his entire life at the edge of his territory, where unseen threats lurk behind every bush.

Even though a cat may never encounter a predator in his entire life, the smell of a litter box (like the smell of a "scent barrier" in the wild) makes many cats extremely nervous. Prowling from room to room as if caged, constantly sniffing the air for danger, a cat can easily become so tense that the slightest stimulus will trigger exaggerated reactions, ones that nearly every cat owner has seen without realizing that the source of the problem is the cat's own litter box.

Left untreated, this condition can lead to a variety of neurotic behavior patterns:

Unrestrained jumping onto high shelves or hiding in dark spaces. When under stress, most cats will first try to expand their territory by exploring every possible space, jumping onto high bookshelves, crawling beneath the kitchen sink, into the washer or dryer, or even into a grocery bag that slips to the floor — any place where the smell of the litter box is reduced. Though many owners consider this to be "cute," it is, in fact, the result of territorial stress.

Excessive face rubbing, constant grooming, incessant meowing. Inundated by the constant smell of a litter box, many cats can no longer smell the scent marks they make by face rubbing. In fact, no matter how much face rubbing they do, they never manage to build up any kind of recognizable scent. As a result, they constantly rub on every available surface, grooming themselves to compensate for the excess dirt they pick up, and meowing more than usual to express their frustration.

Prolonged withdrawal. A cat constantly on edge will often appear aloof and sulky, even going so far as to turn his back when you call him. Though often explained as an example of a cat's "solitary" nature, this kind of withdrawal is another result of territorial stress. Fearful of the danger that the smell of his litter box represents, a cat will feel intimidated by the slightest hostile action—even a pair of staring eyes. Thus, a cat under stress will show his inferiority by turning his back, avoiding the hostile image.

Occasional "mad dashes" around the house. One of the most common ways a cat displays territorial distress is to suddenly run through the house as if he were being chased by the devil, then stop abruptly, look around, and freeze in place. Usually described as a form of "feline exercise" or "overflow behavior," or as a way of expressing his need to hunt and chase prey, the "mad dash" is a perfectly normal reaction when a cat finds himself in the middle of his "scent barrier." Since cats in the wild usually urinate or defecate near the edges of their territory,

where they are in most danger, they will often finish their duties by suddenly arching their backs, emitting a loud throaty sound, and running madly toward the nest in a stiff sideways gait — exactly the way many housebound cats behave after using the litter box.

Sudden fits of anger and/or retaliation. Any change in atmosphere or routine, no matter how small, becomes a catastrophe for a pet living under territorial stress, causing the cat to lash out by scratching or giving up his litter box.

Neurotic behavior. Occasionally a cat will be so overcome by the smell of his litter box that he will become a slave to it. When this happens, the cat will spend as much (or more) time at the box than he does at his food dish — sniffing, digging, moving the litter from one side to another, sometimes transferring the litter from the box to the floor, then using the box as a place to sleep, all but oblivious to the smell of it.

The similarity between these kinds of behavior in a housebound cat and the nervousness that a free-ranging cat experiences near the edge of his territory is no coincidence. Yet the housebound cat cannot escape the smell of his litter. So rather than dirty the box even more, the cat does the only sensible thing possible: he stops using the box altogether. Then where *does* the cat go?

A Comedian's Cat

Lee Frank, a professional comic who lives in New York, toilet trained his cat Bill nearly seven years ago.

"I had to find a way of avoiding the smell every time I came home," he says today. "It was particularly bad after an out-of-town engagement. I could smell it as soon as I left the elevator on my way to the apartment."

Bill was nearly seven years old when training began, but according to Frank, he adjusted rapidly. Using the Alternate Method, Frank raised the litter box next to the toilet, placed a spare toilet seat on top of the box and used a commercial plastic liner instead of plastic wrap during the final phase. "I cut a hole in the liner and made it wider and wider until Bill learned to use the seat instead of the litter," he recalls. "It couldn't have been easier."

Now fourteen years old, Bill has no problem jumping up and balancing on the seat. "When he becomes a little creaky," says Frank, "I plan to build some steps or maybe a ramp next to the toilet so that he can jump up and down more easily."

The only thing Frank hasn't figured out is how to teach Bill to flush when he's finished. "He doesn't like to go when the toilet is dirty," Frank reports. "So, when I'm away, I have a neighbor come in every few hours to flush the toilet."

CASE STUDY

BRIAN COATES

ROOM WITH A MEW

As long as it's clean and relatively quiet, most house cats wind up in the most logical place of all: the bathroom. After that, there's no getting rid of them. Even though cats drink very little water themselves, they seem to enjoy the sound of running or dripping water, and will often drink from an open tap. For this reason, cats have been known to curl up in the bathroom sink (perfect for taking an afternoon nap), drink from the toilet (which, to a cat, is a veritable waterfall that runs at intervals throughout the day), and relieve themselves in the bathtub directly over the drain.

Compared to the litter box, a bathtub drain diffuses the odor of urine so completely that most owners have no idea their cat is doing it in the tub until one day they discover a piece of solid evidence. Given their natural affinity for porcelain fixtures, most cats can use a toilet quite as easily — if properly trained. Their superb balance and natural spread-legged stance make them well suited to the task. All they need is a little guidance and encouragement.

The only requirements for toilet training are that the cat be large enough to jump up onto the toilet (at least six months of age) and thoroughly litter trained. Should you want to toilet train a new kitten, or an older cat that needs retraining, chapter 2 — discusses the correct foundation on which you and your cat can build.

2

THE ART OF THE BOX

By the time a kitten is old enough to leave his mother, he should already have learned how to use a litter box by watching his mother and littermates bury their wastes in the proper way. Therefore, in most cases, all you have to do with a new kitten is place him in the litter after his first feeding, and he will automatically know what to do.

Yet not all kittens remain with their mother long enough to be litter trained. If this is the case with your kitten, you will have to become the kitten's "mother" and train him to use the box yourself. *Remember, you must make sure that your kitten is completely secure in using his litter box — and uses it every time — before you begin toilet training.*

Fortunately litter training is a snap for most kittens, because cats are such inherently clean animals. Before you begin litter training, however, you will need to make sure that the kitten is healthy. For this, you will need to take the cat and a stool sample to a veterinarian so the doctor can test for internal parasites or worms. It's impossible to litter train or toilet train if the cat or kitten has parasites or is ill. While you're at it, make sure the kitten has received, or at least begun, the innoculations necessary to protect him from distemper or feline leukemia (your veterinarian can provide details).

To begin litter training, you will need three items: a litter box, tools to clean and maintain the box, and, of course, an ample supply of cat box filler.

BOXES, BOXES, BOXES

Touring your local pet store, you will find more species of litter box than you ever thought possible, from sleek stainless steel and rustic oak to elaborate contraptions modeled after Hitler's bunker, with a

round hole through which the cat enters and exits.

But don't be fooled. No matter what you may hear, you don't need anything fancy to litter train a cat. The most common litter box is a simple plastic tub, two inches deep, 14 inches wide by 20 inches long. Whatever type of box you choose, make sure that it's stable enough to remain in place when the cat puts his full weight on the edge. If the box ever tips over while the cat is using it, he may never use it again.

Before you decide where to put the box, remember that cats are quite particular about where they do their business. Despite their reputation as creatures of habit, you can't just put the box anywhere.

- Don't place it in the pantry or laundry room. Otherwise, you run the risk of your cat sniffing or eating detergents or other potentially toxic chemicals.

- Don't put the box in the garage. It's too chilly and drafty and exposes the cat to other hazards, such as antifreeze (a sweet-tasting but deadly poison that collects under parked cars).

- Don't place the litter box anywhere near the kitchen. As a rule cats prefer to do their business as far away from their food as possible. In fact, most cats will positively refuse to relieve themselves near where they eat.

In general, you should choose a clean, quiet, well-ventilated spot that is warm in winter, cool in summer, and always available but away from heavy traffic. Most cats will avoid a box that is constantly underfoot. Also, the area around the box should be both out of sight and easy to clean.

As you know, many cats like to spread the litter around as they dig. For this reason, many people keep their cat box in the bathtub, hidden behind the shower curtain, where the litter won't migrate too far.

An even better place for the litter box is next to the toilet, in the corner next to the wall. This setup is ideal for both the cat (it's always available, away from where he eats and sleeps) and you (it's easy to clean and perfect if you eventually want to toilet train the cat). If you have a spare bathroom which is not used by every member of the household, that's even better. Just be sure to keep the bathroom door open. Remove all dangerous or breakable objects from the room, and remember to roll any loose toilet paper into a tight roll so that none of it is left dangling about. Otherwise, the cat will soon have the entire roll on the floor. It's also smart to leave a few catnip toys about, at least for a few days, to make sure the kitten keeps coming back. This way, the bathroom will soon become your cat's favorite spot.

Once you've decided where to put the box, you should think about what to put in it.

CAT BOX FILLER

Since litter training will only be an intermediate step to the ultimate goal of a toilet-trained cat, you should avoid using expensive heavily scented, chemically treated cat box filler. Why? Cats, being creatures of habit, often become attached to the smell of their litter and will miss it once it is removed. In addition, the active ingredients in certain brands of litter may be unsafe. Since cats usually inhale quartz dust (a known carcinogen) and ingest the litter's active ingredients (including artificial fragrances, antimicrobial agents, dyes, etc.) when they lick their paws after digging in the box, you may be risking health problems by using a chemically treated litter (see chapter 3). In general, the fewer chemicals, the better.

If you live near a beach or sandy area, don't be tempted to use sand; it may be free, but eventually the cat will track it all over the house. Try not to use shredded newspapers, either. Even though many pet stores swear by it, the ink in most newsprint contains traces of heavy metals, such as lead and mercury, which are toxic to cats as well as humans.

Since cat box filler is a regional product, with

brands in one area that may not be available in another, you may have to look around to find a good nonchemical filler such as Zodiac® or Everclean. According to Dr. Dale Olm, at the New York ASPCA, "kittens prefer a softer, sandier texture to a granular clay texture. It doesn't smell as much, it's easier for a kitten to dig, and it's *much* easier to clean, since wastes tend to stay in discrete clumps that are easy to remove, thus leaving the surrounding litter clean and odor free."

CLEANING TOOLS

To keep the box as clean as possible, all you *really* need is a giant metal spoon, with no holes or slots in it, kept somewhere near the litter box so that it's always available. Whenever you pass the bathroom, you can check the litter box, quickly grabbing your spoon, collecting the offending matter in a single scoop, and flushing it down the toilet.

BASIC LITTER BOX TRAINING

If your kitten is extremely young, remember that he is still a baby. And as with all babies, you must supervise him until he is old enough to do things on his own. Kittens mature quickly, so the supervision phase rarely lasts longer than two or three weeks.

The basics of litter training are simple but should be followed to the letter to avoid setting your kitten off on the wrong foot. As soon as you bring the kitten home, let him take a good sniff around his new home and scent-mark a few areas by rubbing his face and body against whatever is at hand. Then try to feed him sometime within the first hour or two.

If the cat is not yet accustomed to solid food, try a little *slightly* warm milk, or whatever he will accept; then, once he's finished, wait a moment for the food to settle, then lift him *gently* with your palm under his belly and take him to the bathroom, where the box has been prepared next to the toilet. (Holding the kitten in this way with your warm hand will stimulate the urogenital reflex, the same way his mother did by licking the kitten's belly.)

Close the bathroom door and place the kitten *gently* into the box and keep him there until he has done his business. Be as quiet as possible so that the kitten will not be frightened or nervous. If you have children in the house, make sure they understand the importance of being absolutely silent. Don't say anything; just watch.

If he's already been box trained by his mother, he'll know exactly what to do. After all, he's just eaten and his tiny one-inch-long digestive tract can't hold out forever. You can tell if your kitten is about to urinate or defecate because he will begin to circle round and round with a worried expression, then suddenly crouch, with his tail slightly raised, his eyes closed, and his mouth spread in a devilish little grin.

If he jumps out of the box, *gently* pick him up, hold him with your fingers under his belly for a few seconds, and put him back in the box. Remember, say nothing. The kitten should learn to eliminate on his own without associating his action with the sound of your voice.

After a few minutes, if the kitten still doesn't get the message, reach into the box and let him sniff your hand to reestablish contact. (Remember, you're his mother now, so don't make any sudden or uncertain movements.)

Gently take the cat's right paw using your index finger and thumb and make a scratching motion, moving a few granules of litter. Then release the paw and wait. No matter how much he meows, no matter how pathetic he looks, you must keep him in the box until he performs properly.

If all else fails, you might recall that in the wild mother cats induce their kittens to eliminate by turning them over and licking their stomachs. You can achieve the same effect with your index finger moistened with a little warm water.

Above all, don't push or coerce the kitten or make any nervous sounds or gestures—he simply won't understand. If it's any consolation, this is the hardest part of training a kitten. But once the kitten learns to use the box, he will have cleared a major hurdle.

After this first encounter with the box, let the kitten explore at will. Chances are good that he will return to the box once or twice while making his rounds —which will help orient him before he eats again.

The second time he eats, watch him carefully. If he goes to the box himself, after seemingly aimless wandering, you can rejoice. If instead he starts sniffing around in one spot, turns round and round, then squats with his tail up, *gently* pick him up, take him to the bathroom and keep him there until he does his business. Chances are you won't have to repeat the front paw scratching. Once he knows where he is, the kitten will do his thing right away.

LITTER TRAINING SCHEDULE

How do you know when it's time to place the kitten in the box? Usually, a kitten that can't find his box will start to meow or cry when he needs to go, then start to circle as though looking for his tail. Generally you should assume that a kitten will have to use his box after every meal, after he sleeps, after a bout of strenuous play, and after he chews on something for a long period of time (the act of chewing stimulates the kitten's digestion). Remember that cats, being carnivores with a short intestine and an efficient pair of kidneys, can't hold their wastes very long. Therefore, at the very least, you should place a new kitten in the litter box first thing in the morning, after every meal, and the last thing at night—as well as keeping an eye on him until he starts using the box himself.

Once this pattern is established, your kitten will continue to use his box for the next several months—or at least until he is old enough to start toilet training.

For an older cat moving indoors for the first time, litter training is the same as for a kitten. But remember, whether the cat is young or old, easy to handle or difficult, you should *always* be patient and handle a cat gently and with kindness.

CLEANING THE LITTER BOX

Since the litter box is an integral part of your cat's life and environment, it must receive a lot of attention. Many an owner has successfully untrained a litter-trained cat by forgetting to clean and change the litter on a regular schedule. Indeed, many cats won't go anywhere near a dirty box. At its most extreme, a dirty box can serve as host to a dazzling variety of organisms, including parasites and worm larvae that pass through a cat's feces, hatch, then reinfect your cat—not to mention your children, other pets, and even you. Therefore, it is imperative that you keep the box clean at all times. It may not be the most pleasant of chores but, like taking out the trash, it must be done — at least until your cat has been toilet trained.

The secret to maintaining a clean box is not to use too much cat box filler. First sprinkle a little baking soda in the bottom of the box, then fill it with *one inch* of litter — just enough to permit your cat to scratch and cover his wastes, but no more. Ideally you want the urine to form a clump at the bottom of the box, not spread around and cause the entire box to smell.

To keep odor to a minimum, however, you must be vigilant. Whenever you pass the bathroom, take a quick look at the box. If you see a covered mound, take your large metal spoon and transfer the mound to the toilet. If you see a little wet spot which looks like the tip of a tiny iceberg, lift the box and gently shake all the dry litter to one end exposing the wet clump, remove it with your spoon, and flush. Shake the box to redistribute the litter and rinse the spoon with hot water. If you're careful, the remaining litter will be clean and uncontaminated.

At a minimum, you should check the box when you wake up and when you go to bed. If you're going to be gone for more than a few hours, be sure to check the litter box just before you leave and check it again after you return.

When emptying the box at the end of the week,

rinse it out and dry it thoroughly before putting in the new litter. Cleaning will be a breeze, because you've already scooped up every wet clump as soon as it appeared. At the most there will be an odd speck of dried feces here or there, nothing more. If you use a disinfectant, make sure it is a mild one with little odor. Strong odors will immediately turn off the cat.

Most important: Litter trays should be washed separately from any other household items. Pregnant women should *never* handle a litter box because of the risk of toxoplasmosis (a single-celled parasite often found in cat feces), which can cause birth defects.

If you consider this too much work, remember, it takes only ten seconds to check a litter box. Checking the pan several times a day means that you will need to change and wash the whole pan only once a week. Besides, within a month or two, you will be on the way to toilet training, which will eliminate the box entirely. Every scoop now will save a thousand scoops later.

THE SIX DON'TS OF LITTER TRAINING

Don't listen to cat experts who tell you to keep the litter box "a little dirty" during the kitten's orientation period so that the scent will attract the kitten. This is not only wrong, it's an excellent way of encouraging your cat to turn away from the box and do his business elsewhere.

Follow the Leader

When Ronald and Rose Morin decided to toilet train their three cats Gemma, Teddy, and Sebastian, they were surprised how quickly the cats made the change after Sebastian, the dominant male, first did it. Since their first month together, Gemma and Teddy had always been shy and retiring compared to their brother. "Sebastian was always the first to get into everything," says Mrs. Morin, who breeds Persians at her home in Manchester, New Hampshire.

When the time came to toilet train her own pets, she says, "I decided to concentrate on training Sebastian and hoped that the others would follow along." Each cat was about a year old, and all had been using the same litter box next to the toilet since birth. "Since Sebastian jumped up onto the toilet all the time," she says, "we didn't have to raise the litter box slowly, the way most people do." Instead, she wedged a plastic basin into the center of the toilet seat, sprinkled it with litter and let nature take its course.

"Jumping up onto the toilet seat was no problem for Gemma and Teddy once Sebastian showed them it was OK," she reports. But slipping was something of a problem, partly because the cats' long fur sometimes tucked under their paws. "To give them a better grip," Rose says, "Ronald tied pieces of carpet onto the toilet seat with soft ribbons."

The most delicate moment came when she removed the carpet and put away the litter box. "I was terrified that they wouldn't understand," she recalls. "But, just as before, Gemma and Teddy let Sebastian jump up first and watched him do his thing right there on the rim." Once he was finished, the other two, in turn, jumped up and did likewise.

"During the final phase of the training, it was easy to remove the clumps of Everclean® and flush them down the toilet," she added. The Morins found that Everclean®, unlike most brands of litter, did not clog up their septic tank.

Has toilet training changed their cats' disposition? "Not at all. They seem to treat the toilet the same way they did the litter box. The only difference is that now they don't spread the litter around. Cleaning up after them couldn't be easier."

Don't make the mistake of putting too much litter in the box or using a box that is too large. In general, a box filled with ten pounds of litter will be smellier than a box filled with one pound or two. Why? Because the cat's urine is not allowed to reach the bottom and form a clump. With no clump to scoop out, the smell of urine will continue to permeate the whole ten pounds like a miasmic fog. Despite what you may read on the package, when the litter box begins to smell, try using *less* rather than more.

Don't line your litter box with plastic liners that you may find in pet stores. Plastic liners inevitably form little wrinkles that allow wet litter to hide (and stink to high heaven) no matter how well you shake the box during cleaning. Also, many cats like to claw (and even chew) soft plastic bags. Beware!

Don't buy one of those commercial slotted spoons for cleaning the litter box. Such a spoon may have been fine for serving green beans at your old high school cafeteria, but it's worthless for handling dirty litter, particularly those noxious little clumps that are the worst problem of all.

Don't use green chlorophyll-scented cat box filler, no matter how much you enjoy the smell yourself. Veterinarians will tell you that most cats hate the smell of chlorophyll or pine. Even the Oil-Dri Corporation of America, which introduced the first green chlorophyll-scented cat litter, Litter Green®, admits that most cats don't like it. "It's not a big seller," said the Oil-Dri spokesman.

Don't use any strong cleansers, disinfectants, or spray deodorants. Not only are they unnecessary, most cats hate the smell of strong chemicals and will even stop using the box while the smell is present.

Remember: the first time your cat sets foot in his new home, you must *show* him where to find the litter box, and make sure it is available at all times. Once he recognizes it, the kitten will definitely use the litter box you provide — at least until he is old enough to begin toilet training.

"ACCIDENTS"

No matter how hard you try, most kittens will have an occasional "accident." After all, they are babies. Should your cat do his thing in an inappropriate spot — that is, anywhere but the litter box — it is essential that you remove all evidence of the offense immediately, or the kitten will be attracted to that spot again. Soiled areas should be cleaned as thoroughly as possible and sprayed with a commercial odor neutralizer such as Nilodor or Nature's Miracle (following the instructions on the package), available in most pet stores, or white cider vinegar followed by

plain seltzer and a shake or two of ground black pepper to make sure that the cat does not return. As an added precaution, try covering the spot with a large bulky object, such as a chair or a leafy potted plant. If he persists in using the spot, place his food bowl directly over his last offense and keep it there until the kitten returns to using the litter box, making certain that you always keep his litter box available and scrupulously clean.

No matter what happens, you should never physically punish a cat for not using its litter box. Not only is it cruel, it's also counter-productive. Strike a cat once and he will never trust you again. Scream at him and he may never listen again. As a rule, successful housebreaking is accomplished by prevention, not punishment.

"PROBLEM" CATS

If you encounter extreme difficulties training your kitten to use a litter box, or find that your cat has repeated "accidents," you should know that a certain (albeit small) percentage of domestic cats simply cannot be litter trained. Occasionally this problem stems from being abandoned too soon by their mothers. Growing up wild, these kittens are not suited to domestic life. More often, however, problems with the litter box are the result of excessive inbreeding. Certain strains of Persian cats, for example, seem to have lost their inherent desire for cleanliness.

Ordinarily, a cat that refuses to be litter trained will be difficult for the rest of his life. Therefore, if you find yourself saddled with a "problem" cat, you should decide whether it's better to keep the kitten and suffer or find him a better home, a nearby farm perhaps, where he can live a more natural life. Under no circumstances should you ever abandon a cat, for any reason. Nor should you take him to an animal shelter until you have investigated every possible alternative. Remember, it is your responsibility to find your friend a good home, where he can live the rest of his life in peace.

Once you have succeeded in litter training your cat, you might be so thrilled that you wonder whether it's worth the trouble to toilet train as well. After all, the cat is using the box every time, isn't he? And cleaning up every day or two isn't *that* much of a problem. Right? So, you ask, why fix something when it isn't broken?

Read on . . .

3

THE
MYSTERY OF
THE BOX

O ften when a cat stops using his litter box, the first
thing an owner does is clean up the mess, then run
to the grocery store shelf, where he is confronted
with every scent, texture, color, and flavor known to
modern science. Laced with cryptic additives such as
Sanatac®, Green Gard®, or HealthGuard™ in pressure-
sensitive and moisture-activated granules, scented with
pine oil, baby powder, or mint, modern cat litter is
more than just dirt in a bag. Whether you're in need
of Control®, the reassurance of Everclean® or Tidy
Cat®, the cute cuddly quality of Kitty Diggin's®, or
the up-market connotations of Glamour Kitty®, each
can be found in distinctive yet tasteful packaging
designed for maximum store visibility.

With more than seventy brands to choose from,
America's thirty million-plus cat owners sift their way

through more than 1.8 million *tons* of litter every year — enough to fill the 102-story Empire State Building from the deepest subterranean passage to the top of the observation deck *two and one-half times* — in a market that will soon reach five hundred million dollars nationwide. After dragging this dirt home every week, storing it, pouring it, and checking it for lumps every day, the loving cat owner must finally dispose of this mess in the garbage, where it enters the waste stream bound for the nearest open landfill. All for an animal that rarely expresses much gratitude.

When did this madness begin? Forty-three years ago, on a cold January morning in Cassopolis, Michigan, when Kay Draper discovered that the sandpile she used to fill her cat's litter box had frozen solid. According to legend, Mrs. Draper went to see her neighbor, Edward Lowe, who was struggling to rescue

his father's ice-hauling business. Did he have anything she could use to fill her cat's box?

Scratching his chin, Lowe searched through the trunk of his 1943 Chevy and came up with a bag of granulated clay that he had been trying to sell as nesting material to local chicken farmers.

She tried it, came back for another bag, and soon had every cat owner in town calling for more. Within a few weeks, Lowe was making regular deliveries of granulated clay packed in little brown bags, which he called "Kitty Litter."

Today Edward Lowe's Kitty Litter® and Tidy Cat 3® brands, which together dominate the cat box filler industry with more than $110 million in yearly sales, are the subject of intense testing and refinement. In the secret laboratories of Golden Cat Corporation, the makers of all Edward Lowe products, researchers in white coats conduct round-the-clock surveillance — analyzing miles of videotape taken from cameras that scan every inch of Golden Cat's supersecret glass-enclosed cattery — testing their filler against every other brand on the market to determine the precise combination of scent, color, and texture that appeals most to a cat's nose and paw. Meanwhile, dozens of hard-faced professional "sniffers" evaluate variously soiled litters in elaborate double-blind studies, straining to describe the throat-catching stench as the samples age at room temperature.

Using this information, Golden Cat technicians formulate and refine their top-secret fragrances, disinfectants, deodorants, germicides, antifungal, antiparasitic, and antibacterial agents into that "exciting, yet subtle new fragrance" that will kill the odor a cat makes without killing the cat that makes it.

WHAT'S REALLY *IN* CAT LITTER?

In the forty-three years since Edward Lowe founded a million-dollar industry out of the trunk of his car, manufacturers have been lured by the low costs and high profits associated with cat litter, using every conceivable absorbant material — including oat flakes, alfalfa chaff, corn cobs, and orange peels — to make what cats do in their boxes as pleasant and odor free as possible.

Yet of all known materials, the substance most widely used in commercial cat litter is fuller's earth, a highly porous diatomaceous clay that attracts and absorbs virtually any liquid that flows in its direction. Used for more than seven thousand years, longer than any other mineral except flint, fuller's earth has a variety of industrial, medicinal, and cosmetic uses. For example, a close cousin of fuller's earth, kaolin, is a primary ingredient in the antidiarrheal Kaopectate.

The largest known deposit of fuller's earth, formed more than two hundred million years ago, when

Africa separated from North America, lies today along the eastern border of Florida and Georgia. Here and at other deposits in Mississippi, Louisiana, California, and Oregon, the fat cats of the cat box filler industry operate immense open-pit mining operations. Using steam shovels the size of apartment buildings, they scoop dirt into enormous dump trucks, which transport their loads to giant automated factories where the clay is pulverized, screened to precise tolerances, washed, and sterilized in tumbling ovens that resemble oversized cement mixers.

Once this earth has cooled and the dust settled, each maker adds its own secret blend of odor-eating, pressure- and moisture-sensitive chemical additives.

Encased in a thin membrane of food starch that dissolves when moistened, the tiny blue, green, and red pellets found in Kitty Litter® — not unlike the patented formulas in Fresh Step® and Control® — contain some of the most highly concentrated chemical additives found in any consumer product. According to Clay Nelson, chief of research and development at Golden Cat, every *ton* of pulverized, screened, and sanitized clay used in Kitty Litter®, contains *one pound* of Healthguard™, starch-encapsulated fragrances, deodorants, dyes, and disinfectants. This means that a litter box with sixteen ounces of Kitty Litter® actually contains 15.992 ounces of clay and only *8/1,000th of an ounce* of Healthguard™. Never in the history of marketing has so little been entrusted to do so much.

What are these chemicals?

"Our list of ingredients is proprietary," says Clay Nelson adding that "all Edward Lowe products are thoroughly tested" and that "no Edward Lowe product has ever harmed any cat."

Would he make any of these safety tests available?

"No," he replies after a short pause, "the test results are also proprietary."

Indeed, determining the precise ingredients of any cat box filler is difficult, if not impossible, in part because the materials that litter makers purchase from chemical specialty firms and fragrance houses such as International Flavors and Fragrances are themselves secret.

Since cats routinely ingest these chemicals every time they use the litter box, dissolving the starch-covered capsules with their urine, hiding the spot, then licking their paws afterward, many cat owners and veterinarians question whether something strong enough to subdue the odor of a pound of sodden feces-laden litter isn't also strong enough to subdue the cat.

According to Bill McCormick, chief toxicologist at the Clorox company's cat litter research center in Pleasonton, California, thousands of man-hours have been spent on palatability studies for the company's number-one seller, Fresh Step® (the brand that "Freshens With Every Step®"). Even though the package clearly states that "Fresh Step® has been safety tested by independent laboratories," those tests refer to acute reactions of *humans* exposed to Fresh Step® in the factory, not chronic effects on cats.

"To my knowledge, no manufacturer has ever released safety data on the chronic effect of litter on the cats that use it," says McCormick.

According to the Material Safety Data Sheet that Clorox filed with the OSHA (the Occupational Safety and Health Administration in Washington, D.C.), Fresh Step® contains three "hazardous ingredients," including the unidentified fragrance ("exposure limit not established"). One of the ingredients, silica, "may be carcinogenic" to animals and humans, according to the International Association for Research in Cancer. The Data Sheet acknowledges this.

The most common way that foreign substances invade a cat's body is by inhalation — the cat using its supersensitive nose where perhaps it shouldn't. According to the Fresh Step® Material Safety Data Sheet, "inhalation [by humans] . . . may irritate nose and throat . . . [and] prolonged or repeated exposure may cause cough, shortness of breath, scarring of the lung and cancer."

Additionally, because of their fastidious nature, cats

are likely to swallow anything that gets onto their fur or paws, passing it through the stomach and intestines, where the fat-soluble additives in litter enter the bloodstream and lodge themselves in the cat's fatty tissue. In this way, a large yet unknown variety of agents can build up, year after year, slowly attacking the cat's vital organs while debilitating his nervous system.

In its later stages, chronic exposure to substances such as **PVP** (polyvinyl pyrolidine, a potent antimicrobial iodine compound which the **EPA** has authorized for use in Kitty Litter® in a private consent agreement) has been linked to a chemically induced feline immune deficiency reaction known as **FAIDS**, an insidious condition not unlike human **AIDS**, that is as difficult to diagnose as it is to treat. According to a source familiar with Environmental Protection Agency documents, the amount of titratable iodine in Kitty Litter® is so small (and hence, presumably, potent) that only two-tenths of a pound are needed per *ton* of litter to achieve the desired effect.

IS CAT LITTER BAD FOR YOUR CAT?

Legally, manufacturers that sell products meant for use by animals are not required to publish the same health and safety data that the Food and Drug Administration requires for products intended for human consumption. Therefore, the likelihood of ever knowing the true effect of cat litter on feline health is as small as the amount of titratable iodine in a mountain of Kitty Litter®.

Faced with a shelf in their local grocery store packed full of promises wrapped in bright packages, each making its own miraculous claims, most cat owners assume (or at least hope) that phrases like "safety tested by independent laboratories" means that the product is "safe." Yet researchers and veterinarians specializing in the science of immunotoxicology — the long-term effects of exposure to low-grade toxins, poisons, and environmental pollutants — believe many common substances can slowly undermine a cat's urinary, nervous, and immune systems when potent dosages are administered in tiny amounts over a long period of time.

"As the cat's condition worsens," notes Debra Pirotin, a New York veterinarian, "it is sometimes difficult to see that the cat is really ill. Often the only indications of systemic poisoning are gradual weight loss with secretions from the eye and nose and general listlessness." With their defenses impaired, many cats quickly succumb to the first opportunistic infection, says Dr. Pirotin. These include FCV (*feline calcici virus*) and FVR (*feline viral rhinotracheitis*), viruses that were once rare but are now quite common.

The role of chemical contamination in this situation is still uncertain. Nonetheless, cat owners have begun to turn away from chemically treated litter to such an extent that Golden Cat is rumored to be working on a new "litter-free" cat box using a disposable absorbent material, not unlike a disposable baby diaper, instead of cat box filler.

Now that you are familiar with the reasons why your cat should not be using a litter box, try to read all of chapter 4 before starting the 21-Day Program.

4

21 DAYS TO A LITTER-FREE CAT

A
s we know, the potential for learning exists inside every cat. In fact, behind that impenetrable gaze, *most* cats are easy to teach. Though dormant, their capacity for learning lies just beneath the surface, like a vast mineral deposit just waiting to be tapped. If your cat is like most, the next three weeks will be a breeze.

Yet for certain cats, the idea of changing even the simplest behavior is like looking for a diamond in a mountain of gravel. If this is your cat, what should you do? How do you find the diamond? You don't. You let the cat find it for you.

Unlike conventional training, in which an animal is taught to respond to an outside stimulus (the threat of pain or the promise of a reward), the 21-Day Program employs a form of behavior modification that takes full advantage of your cat's intelligence and flexibility. You do half of the work, and your cat does the other half.

The object is to induce a new form of "chaining" behavior through progressive modification — gradually altering the environment in which the old behavior was expressed by shifting the height, position, and size of the litter box vis à vis the toilet until box and toilet become one. Unlike conventional training, which is only effective when the animal is paying full attention, progressive modification works no matter what your cat's mood happens to be.

More important, the 21-Day Program does not require the cat to do anything outside of his normal repertoire. While using the toilet, your cat will balance himself, squat on his hind legs, and expel in virtually the same way he would in a litter box, garden, or open field. The physical behavior is essentially the same, only the setting is different.

Your job as the cat's trainer is to break down the change of circumstances into a series of small, comprehensible steps—tiny hurdles that are so insignificant that your cat will naturally accommodate himself in order to maintain the status quo. Each time your cat departs from his previous pattern in response to the next hurdle, following a predetermined path, he establishes a new link in what eventually becomes an entirely new "chain" of behavior. This "chaining" phenomenon is a fundamental aspect of feline psychology and the key to the success of the 21-Day Program.

Virtually any adolescent or adult male or female can learn to use a toilet instead of a litter box as long as the cat is neutered (don't even *attempt* to train an unaltered cat!), completely litter trained (using the box in the bathroom, next to the toilet), and capable of jumping sixteen inches from the floor in a single leap. Once you are certain that your cat is using the litter box when placed next to the toilet, your objective will be to construct a new chain of behavior that your cat can master one link at a time. Like any other skill, toilet training takes time and practice. So no matter how enthusiastic your cat might appear in the early phase, don't rush. For the technique to be effective, your cat will need plenty of time to replace the memory of his old behavior with the new behavior chain that he is learning.

The first link in this chain will be to raise the box one or two inches per day—slowly coaxing the cat to *step* up, *hop* up, and finally *jump* up in order to use

the box. Then, as the box is slowly raised to the same
level as the toilet and the act of jumping has been
thoroughly mastered, you will continue the chain by
allowing the cat to become accustomed to the toilet
seat, giving him enough time to explore its solid surface and use it as a platform for jumping up and down.

Within ten days to fourteen days, the cat will come
to trust this new arrangement enough for you to add
the next link in the chain: introducing an obstacle that
will inspire the cat to position himself *over* the litter
by balancing on the edge of the toilet seat rather than
standing in the litter itself.

Coaxing the cat to balance on the seat as soon as
possible is the key to successful toilet training. Turning that key, however, is not always easy.

STANDARD METHOD

Once the litter box has been raised to the same
height as the toilet seat, most cats will take to using
the toilet seat within two or three days. Thus, following the Standard Method, you can dispense with the
litter box next to the toilet, substituting a miniature
box that you attach to the porcelain rim just below
the toilet seat. (This miniature box is easy to set up,
remove when someone needs to use the bathroom,
and dispose of after the cat has done his business.)

ALTERNATE METHOD

If, on the other hand, your cat seems slow or resistant to change, you may want to use an alternate method, in which you raise the litter box to the same level as the toilet seat and keep it there for several days. During this period, you will construct the same miniature box as described in the Standard Method. At the same time, you will attach a spare toilet seat *on top of* the raised litter box and manipulate this arrangement until the cat discovers how easy it is to use the litter by balancing on the spare toilet seat — taking as much time as the cat requires to get it right. Once this occurs, you can safely remove the litter box, while retaining the miniature litter box located beneath the real toilet seat next door.

After the cat begins to use the miniature litter box beneath the toilet seat, you will gradually eliminate the litter until there is none at all. By the end of the twenty-first day, your cat will be so accustomed to jumping up, positioning himself, and balancing on the edge of the toilet seat that he will not even miss the litter. And so long as you give him complete access to his new environment (*always* keeping the bathroom door open and the toilet seat down), he will continue to jump up and position himself as though controlled by automatic pilot.

Without the constant smell of urine and feces filling

his nostrils, your cat will not only look happier and healthier, he will feel like a totally new creature — as though a terrible weight has been lifted from his furry little shoulders. And you, after twenty-one days of minimal effort, can sit back and enjoy the benefits of having a completely toilet-trained cat: no litter to buy, no mess to clean up, and above all, *no smell*!

The vast majority of cats are capable of following the Standard 21-Day Program. For the Standard Method, you will need:

1. A shallow plastic litter box. The box should be twelve to fourteen inches wide by eighteen inches long, reasonably sturdy, but fairly shallow — no more than three or four inches deep. Though a shallow pan might have more spillage than a deep one — particularly if your cat likes to dig and spread the litter around — it is easier for the cat to jump into, and less likely to tip over when raised several inches off the floor. If you can't find a shallow box, use one that's a little deeper. Try to avoid using a box that is more than four inches deep.

2. Enough cat box filler to last for 21 days. If your cat has a favorite brand, continue to use it. If you've been using a heavy scented brand such as Kitty Litter®, Fresh Step®, or Control®, buy an eight-pound bag of that brand, *plus* an eight-pound bag of an un-

scented brand such as Zodiac®, Everclean®, or Hartz Mountain Unscented. Since many cats are literally "hooked" on the smell of their chemically treated litter, it's important to wean them off the smell slowly by using less and less of the chemically treated filler and more and more of the unscented brand. (Soft, fine-grained brands such as Zodiac® or Everclean® are particularly useful, since flushing them down the toilet will not harm your pipes or septic tank.)

3. Books, magazines, newspapers—anything that is wide, flat, and stable—in sufficient quantity to create a stack 14 inches wide, 18 inches long, and 14 to 16 inches high. Since you will be raising the litter box an inch or two per day during the first eight or nine days of the program, you will not need a huge pile of material to begin the program. Yet once you start raising the box, you must continue to raise it (collecting books and magazines as needed) until you've reached the proper height. Don't use anything to support the box that you might need at a moment's notice (such as telephone books).

4. One roll of heavy-duty plastic wrap. Needed to construct a miniature litter box in the center of the toilet seat during the final phase of the program.

5. One roll of wide adhesive tape. Used for securing the plastic wrap to the toilet's porcelain rim.

For the Alternate Method, you will need the same four items . . . plus:

6. A spare toilet seat. An intermediate step that eases the cat's transition from the raised litter box to the toilet, the spare toilet seat (secured on top of the litter box) gives the cat time to practice positioning and balancing himself—before he graduates to the real thing. Spare toilet seats are available at any hardware or home supply store (price: approximately $9.95).

This is all you will need to complete the program. But, before you begin, take a look at your calendar. If you cannot be home for twenty-one consecutive days, put the training off until you have a block of free time. For the 21-Day Program to be successful, you must pay attention to the timing and sequence of details. Starting the 21-Day Program, then leaving in the middle with instructions for your housekeeper, child, or next-door neighbor to follow while you're away is not a good idea.

Barnum & Bailey

· C A S E · S T U D Y ·

When Beverly Moore first laid eyes on Barnum and Bailey eight years ago, the two black-and-white mixed-breed shorthairs were all that remained of a litter of eight kittens. "They had been raised on a ranch near Midland, Texas," says Beverly, a native Texan who now lives in New York City. "And like most range cats, they spent nearly all of their time outside."

Until moving to New York, Beverly had never realized how much work a litter box would be. Buying litter, hauling it home, maintaining the box and disposing of dirty litter became a real burden. "I had heard of toilet training, but I never knew how easy it was," she says.

Using the Standard Method, Beverly trained her cats in less than a month, even though Barnum is a klutz. "Like a lot of big cats, he's always climbing on things and falling because the surface isn't large enough to support him," she admits. "Needless to say, we've become good friends with our veterinarian," she says. Yet the vet didn't know that Beverly's cats were toilet trained until Bailey came down with a bladder infection.

"The vet needed a urine sample, so I took Bailey into the bathroom, and obtained a sample with no problem. The vet," she adds, "was extremely impressed."

If you have an extra bathroom, try to reserve it for your cat during and after training. The reasons are obvious. For one thing, toilet training is a delicate time for your cat; once you begin, nothing should be allowed to disturb or impede his progress. Sharing a bathroom with a pack of bathroom-hoarding teenagers is not the best way to change your cat's most intimate behavior. Nor is it pleasant for a guest (or for you) to find a cat box rising next to the toilet or, later, finding a toilet filled with cat droppings.

Whether or not you have an extra bathroom, it's important that the bathroom be kept as clean and odor-free as possible, with the door *open* and the toilet seat *always* down (with the seat cover up)— even during the first few days, when the cat is using the litter box and not the toilet itself. Having a spare bathroom, one that's not in constant use, will make this somewhat easier. Otherwise, you must be vigilant: an unappealing bathroom, or one that's inaccessible, is the surest way of discouraging your cat from ever making the transition from litter to loo.

GAINING THE UPPER PAW

No matter how hard you try, it's futile to expect a cat to change his most intimate behavior without considerable planning. In fact, convincing a cat to do *anything*—especially something he has never seen before

—can be difficult at best. Therefore, you should not deviate from the details contained in this chapter; nor should you expect the 21-Day Program to work in less than three full weeks.

Since cats are living things subject to an almost infinite number of eccentricities (the same as people), every feline reacts differently to behavior modification. Therefore, when training any animal, remember that every action you take has either a positive or negative effect on your cat's progress. "It's impossible to train a cat, or any pet, until the owner has first trained himself," says Brian Kilcommons, a noted pet trainer, based in New York. "In order to maintain control over the situation, the owner must ensure that every action is fair, firm, and fun."

Fair. If at any time you sense that something is wrong, you should first analyze your own actions. Are you following the program precisely? Is your timing correct? Are you rushing your cat? Are you taking *too much* time between steps? (Forward motion is important here—you don't want to give your cat time to balk or get bored.) Are you cleaning the box every day as usual? Are you giving the right verbal support each time the cat succeeds? Are you confusing the cat with improper commands or gestures? Each can throw even the brightest feline off his stride.

Firm. Assuming that you are following the instructions, are you treating the cat firmly, without compromise? In order for the cat to change his behavior, you must be prepared to enforce the new regime if necessary. But remember that enforcement is not punishment; it's correction. If, for instance, on day eleven, a cat refuses to transfer from box to toilet, try picking him up and placing him on the toilet seat — *gently* so that he will not be frightened or disturbed. You must make certain that your cat knows what's expected — and does it again and again until the new habit takes hold. Praising the desired behavior — and correcting the undesired — will work wonders.

Fun. If you make training enjoyable, you will shorten the time it takes for the cat to learn what you want him to do. "No cat will allow himself to be trained unless he *wants* to do it," Kilcommons observes. "Therefore, you must praise him when he does something right, then praise him again. The harder he works for you, the better."

Whether your cat is bright or somewhat slow, the basics of toilet training are the same for every cat. When in doubt, follow the instructions precisely and be patient.

Keep things simple. Don't let your cat think that anything "new" or "different" is happening. This will only divert the cat from the matter at hand. By keeping things as simple as possible, providing a clear, well-defined problem with only one solution, followed by another problem (with only one solution), and another, you leave little or no room for your cat to make mistakes.

Don't push too fast. Even the smartest cat will become confused or give up if he feels he's being pushed too fast, so don't press beyond your cat's comfort level. Instead of concentrating on the *next* step, concentrate on the present and watch for signs of reluctance or stress. If your cat looks wobbly or erratic, be prepared to retreat one step for every two forward. Sudden changes in training or environment should also be avoided. Remember, as far as a cat is concerned, the best surprise is no surprise.

Make every experience count. Each time your cat interacts with you, he is learning something. When he rubs against your leg and you scratch his ears, he's learning. When he buries his waste in the litter box, then watches you grab your spoon, dig it out, and flush it down the toilet, he's learning. He's learning that you can be directed — that, as far as the litter box is concerned, he's in charge. He is not saying, "Oh, what a helpful owner I have." He's saying, "Oh, what an *obedient* owner I have!" Thus, when he decides to do his thing outside of the box, and watches you immediately clean it up, the pattern is further reinforced.

Therefore, once you decide to toilet train your cat,

you must let him know who is boss. From now on, every time your cat does something right, you must praise him for ten seconds, tell him he is marvelous, then ignore him. This way, the cat will learn to respond to *you*, rather than you responding to the cat. When you pet your cat, make it warm, loving — and brief.

Use commands sparingly and precisely. Since felines do not understand the English language, there's no point explaining things in too much detail. Remember that cats respond more to the *sound* of your voice than the actual words. Once your cat has completed a particular stage of the program, praise him for complying. You want to make this new experience as pleasant for the cat as possible. Most felines look to their owner for approval. Then again . . .

Don't overpraise the cat. Unlike dogs, cats will perform an action only if there is some logical reason for doing so. Unlike a dog, which will do any number of things for

the promise of a subsequent reward, cats are "feel good" creatures, who strive only to enhance their physical and mental comfort.

The more you wait for your cat to perform correctly before you give praise, the more he will work. If the cat comes to expect praise every time he goes to the john, he may not be able to go without it. Who is going to provide the essential words when you're not at home? Using the toilet should be its own reward.

Be reliable. If you want your pet to perform and obey, you must be worthy of his respect. The more reliable you are, the happier your cat will be. Consistency in what you say, how you say it, what you expect, and how you respond makes all the difference when training a cat.

Keep things pleasant. Never reprimand your cat for doing something that is not exactly right; otherwise, he may never do it again. Ideally, you should never use the word "no" if you expect the cat to do something and he does something a little different. Why? Because cats naturally associate the word "no" with a reprimand: "no" when you find him sleeping in the washer/dryer; "no" when he jumps up on the counter; "no" when he jumps in the car and wants to go for a ride. Therefore, when the cat begins to associate the word "no" with whatever you are trying to teach him, he is likely to follow your command and stop or run away. Should he become frightened or hurt himself during training, you can be sure he will never go near a toilet again. One bad experience is all it takes. Failure to secure the litter box to its support (Standard Method) or to secure the spare toilet seat to the litter (Alternate Method) are the two leading causes of accidents while following the 21-Day Program.

Don't get angry. No matter what happens, it's not worth losing your temper. Punishment or the threat of punishment is totally ineffective with cats, because it invokes rebellion rather than submission, or worse, a desire to escape. Remember, cats do most things for their own reasons. If a cat sees some advantage in performing a particular action, he will do it automatically. If not, anger will only make matters worse. Treat your cat poorly and he will dive under the bed.

So, keeping this in mind, let's begin:

DAY

1 Place the shallow litter box on the floor next to the toilet, which from now on will always have the seat down and the seat cover up.** Fill the box with no more than one inch of litter to make cleaning easier and to help control the odor. Remember, boxes with more litter tend to smell worse than those containing less.

DAY

2 Slip one or two magazines or newspapers under the litter box, raising it about half an inch off the floor.** This will force the cat to step up before using the box. Remember to check the box every few hours and clean it thoroughly every other day so that smells do not accumulate.

DAY

3 **Slip another two or three magazines or newspapers under the box, raising it a full inch off the floor.** When choosing titles, think large format. No *TV Guide* or *Reader's Digest*, please. Many cat owners find that *Life* magazine provides the best platform for toilet training. Not only is the size ideal for supporting a litter box, its particular ink and cover stock result in a smooth, slightly tacky surface that minimizes slippage. Others prefer *Vanity Fair* or the *National Enquirer*. Whatever you have around will probably work.

DAYS

4 & **5** **Continue adding magazines and/or newspapers. As you can see, the idea is to slowly raise the box higher and higher until it reaches the height of the toilet.** Elevation rates vary depending on the cat's size, age, and willingness to learn. Most cats love to jump; others are more resistant. Keep in mind that a small kitten can only jump to certain heights until he has had time to grow.

DAY

6 **Keep raising the box.**
By the sixth day, your
cat will probably notice
what you are doing and
put two and two together. Don't
be surprised if he follows you to
the magazine pile, then runs to the
bathroom and watches you slip the
next installment under the litter
box.

By now, he will have to jump a
little to use it, a little higher each
day. But don't worry, the chance
of his rejecting the box because
of height is extremely small. Four
inches isn't much of a barrier, even
for a tiny kitten. As long as the
box remains steady and *clean*, he
will continue to use it.

DAY

7 **Continue raising the
box at the same pace
as before—and be
patient.** Toward the end
of the first week, many owners
try to speed up the process by
raising the box three or four
inches per day—overlooking the
fact that change must be gradual
for the cat to avoid confusion and
develop the trust needed to stay
on track.

If the slow progress seems to
bore you, try focussing on something else, such as the cat box
filler you're using up. If it's a highly
fragranced, chemically treated filler,
your cat will miss the druglike
fragrance if it is suddenly removed,

and that will impede his ultimate move from litter to toilet.

With this in mind, now would be a good time to start weaning your cat from the fragrance by gradually mixing it with an unscented brand such as Everclean®.

Depending on the severity of his dependence, it can take a full two weeks for a cat to withdraw from heavily scented cat box filler. Like the change in height, any change in filler must be gradual. Now that his jumping pattern is well underway, you can begin altering the mixture, using two-thirds scented filler to one-third unscented.

DAY 8

Continue raising the box. Now that it's a full eight to ten inches off the floor, you might consider replacing the stacks of newspapers or magazines with something more solid — woodblocks, bricks, cinderblocks, whatever is at hand — but only if a substitute is readily available, and only if you can continue raising the height *gradually*. Though cats have a superb sense of balance, the box must be stable enough to remain steady every time your cat jumps up to use it.

DAYS

9 & 10

Now that the cat is really jumping, you can safely raise the litter box two inches per day — one inch in the morning, another in the evening — so long as you make sure that the cat uses the box at each new level before raising the box further. If you detect the slightest hint of resistance, hold the box at that level until the resistance subsides. Try not to lower the box, if possible. Once the cat feels secure again, within a day or two, you can resume *slowly* — no more than one inch per day.

Don't forget to clean and change the litter as needed, gradually adjusting the proportion of scented/unscented filler.

DAYS

11 thru 13

Now that the top of the litter box is level with the surface of the toilet seat, raise it another inch or two until the *bottom* of the litter box is at the same level as the toilet seat. Make sure the box is secure on its pile of magazines, books, or bricks, and hold it there for two full days.

Once your cat has reached this exalted height, he will need a little extra time to reinforce the habit of jumping up and down next to the adjoining toilet seat (which should always be *down* with the seat cover *up*). With any luck, he will take time to inspect the toilet seat while doing his business, peer down into the cool waters and even step over the seat as a way of jumping up and down — confirming that it is solid enough to support his entire weight.

Continue cleaning the litter every day. If you are adjusting the filler, you should now be using half scented and half unscented.

Having raised the litter box to the same level as the toilet seat, the next step will be to persuade the cat to balance himself on the toilet seat—a step that fills many owners with visions of their cats falling into the water, grabbing the flusher, and descending into the municipal sewer system. There is no need to worry about a cat slipping off the toilet seat. Now that the jumping/balancing reflex has been thoroughly ingrained, an occasional slip will not deter the cat. Instead it will force him to solve the problem by jumping up

on the other side of the toilet, then leaning against the back of the toilet for support.

Rather than concern yourself with irrational fears, take a moment to rate your cat's progress so far. The purpose of making gradual, incremental changes during the first two weeks of the program is to make sure that the cat reprograms himself to change his behavior every time you change the height of his box. Like any other animal, a cat learns best by association and repetition.

So ask yourself: Has your cat made consistent progress with no objections? Or has he been resistant? Has he taken time to walk around the toilet seat during the past few days, accepting it as part of the litter box? Or has he taken pains to avoid it, always jumping up and down from the other side of the box?

Decisions, Decisions ... With any luck, your cat will have already demonstrated a form of "chaining" behavior—associating a specific sequence of events (looking up, jumping up, balancing, using the litter box, jumping down) with a pleasurable experience. If so, you can continue the 21-Day Program using the Standard Method, designed for cats that accept change with little or no reluctance. The Standard Method is by far the simplest, most straightforward way of completing your cat's toilet training. Many thousands of cats have been trained using variants of the Standard Method in every conceivable situation with very few failures. It works!

If, on the other hand, your cat has been resistant or reluctant to jump higher and higher, he may need a little extra time. In this case, you should follow the Alternate Method, which requires the use of a spare toilet seat placed over the litter box during the final seven days of training. Though it's a bit more trouble (and difficult to explain to guests who might need to use the bathroom), the Alternate Method ensures that your cat

will have enough time to balance and position himself properly *before* you take the final step of removing the box. Followed carefully and diligently, the chance of failure using this Alternate Method is even smaller than with the Standard Method.

Once you have decided which method to follow, take a deep breath and proceed to Day Fourteen.

DAY Standard Method

14

Move the litter box an inch or two toward the toilet seat, so that one-quarter of the box is resting on the toilet itself. As far as the cat is concerned, very little has changed. Positioning the box this way virtually forces him to support himself on the edge of the toilet seat, if only while jumping up and down. Of course, you will have to move the box each time a member of the household wants to use the bathroom. But remember to replace the box in its previous position after every use.

Alternate Method

Remove the spare toilet seat from its package and place it on top of the litter box, with the lid up and the seat down, attaching it securely. You can use any method of holding them together. For most people, using wide adhesive tape around the sides is effective, since it requires no complex hardware and can be easily removed when the box needs to be cleaned. There is no need to remove the toilet seat cover; in fact, it is best to keep it in a raised position just like the real toilet beside it. The idea is to make the litter box and the toilet appear as similar (to the cat) as possible.

Don't be lazy. Many owners fail to anchor the seat to the box properly and thus jeopardize the whole toilet training process. Even though it is quite heavy and feels secure when placed over a box, a loose toilet seat can be easily knocked over by a rambunctious cat, thus ruining all of your progress.

Once your cat begins using the litter box with a toilet seat attached, watch carefully. Presented with this obstacle, most cats will walk round and round the edge of the toilet seat, testing its stability and finally, miraculously, will balance on the edge of the toilet seat, with their posterior over the litter.

If your cat performs correctly, watch to make sure that he does it several times without variation, then proceed to Day Seventeen. If not, don't despair. By squeezing himself into the center of the spare toilet seat rather than balancing himself on the edge, your cat has proven that you were right to select the Alternate Method. Unless he is very small, he will eventually feel cramped and discover a more pleasant way to use the litter on the second or third try. If necessary, wait an entire day and watch from a distance, to see whether he learns to balance on the seat rather than step into the box. Don't confuse the issue by trying to teach him — for the behavior to take hold, the cat **must** decide to balance on the seat himself.

Meanwhile, continue cleaning the box as usual, adding a little less scented and a little more unscented litter.

DAY   Standard Method

15

Move the litter box again, so that three-quarters of it rests on the toilet seat. The rest of the box will remain on the support next to the toilet. As before, the cat will jump up, but this time, he will relieve himself closer to the toilet seat. While using the box, he will note the raised toilet seat cover, the edge of the toilet seat, and the water below—all of these sights associated with the pleasurable experience of relieving himself.

As you continue cleaning the litter, you can now start using two-thirds of the new nonchemical filler and one-third of the cat's old brand.

Alternate Method

Continue watching. If the cat learns to balance himself on the toilet seat, watch to make sure he does it every time he eliminates. (Once you are satisfied that he is doing it again and again, you can proceed to Day Seventeen.

If your cat doesn't seem to be catching on, don't panic. Many cats will learn to balance themselves by the end of the fifteenth or sixteenth day; others take more time. Eventually you may have to nudge him in a manner that allows him to make the move himself. *Remember: your cat must learn to balance by himself, otherwise he is likely to slip back or become confused at a later time.* Too much talk or hovering at this critical moment can easily cause your cat to associate your presence and/or verbal assurances with the act of balancing on the toilet seat. So, stand back and, above all, be patient.

DAY   Standard Method

16
Place the litter box directly over the toilet seat and remove the books, magazines, or bricks you have used to support the box next to the toilet. Secure the litter box with wide adhesive tape placed at strategic points where the box adjoins the porcelain underneath.

Now you can see why it's important to use a shallow litter box. As your cat's landing pad, the litter box will now be subjected to sudden lateral forces every time your cat jumps up and down. Therefore, the box must be anchored securely. Any slip at this point would be disastrous.

Removing the pile of books or magazines next to the toilet will be the biggest change so far. So to make the cat feel more secure, *keep the cat box in this position for at least one full day*—or two days if you detect any confusion or resistance.

During this phase—constantly removing and replacing the cat box each time someone visits the bathroom—your patience may start to wear thin. You may start to question the entire procedure. But don't! Things may look dark, but somewhere down that long tunnel, a bead of light is starting to form.

Alternate Method

If, by the sixteenth day, your cat still persists in squeezing himself into the toilet seat and using the litter directly, now is the time to act. Take a strip of adhesive tape, trim it to a width of one-quarter inch, and stick it under the edge of the toilet seat — across the hole of the toilet seat, directly over the litter — leaving the sticky side exposed.

The next time your cat visits the box, he will notice the obstruction and start to circle round and round the edge of the toilet seat. Since using the litter has been thoroughly ingrained, the cat will continue to circle until, with any luck, he decides that the only way is to balance himself on the edge of the toilet seat.

If this doesn't work and he continues to go inside the box, attach another piece of tape across the box in the other direction. With the second piece of tape, squeezing into the box will be even more difficult. Eventually, he will solve the problem the only way he can. If he seems confused, confine him to the bathroom until he learns to balance and use the litter box/toilet seat properly. Keep the litter box steady to build up his trust.

Occasionally, cats will become confused and start using the *real* toilet by mistake. If this happens, watch the situation carefully to make sure that he is *really* balancing on the seat, before proceeding.

DAY   Both Methods

17

By this time, your cat should be ready to use the toilet itself, without a litter box or spare toilet seat. Therefore, the next four days will be spent reinforcing everything your cat has learned — while reducing his dependence on the smell and texture of litter through a technique known as "successive approximation."

If you are using the Standard Method, you should be certain that your cat is comfortable jumping up and using the litter box while it is on top of the toilet seat. **If you are using the Alternate Method,** your cat should have succeeded in balancing

himself on the spare toilet seat positioned over the litter box. Now is the time to remove the litter box/spare toilet seat (as well as the books and magazines underneath). Put them away and keep them out of sight. Clean the box thoroughly and store it in a cupboard where your cat will not find it. At this point, it's important that he not smell anything associated with the litter box.

Next, lift the toilet seat, take a sheet of plastic wrap and attach the plastic across the toilet's porcelain rim. Many brands of plastic wrap will cling to porcelain, others will not. Reinforce the edges with adhesive tape to be certain.

Leave a slight depression in the plastic as you secure it. Finally, place a cup (or less) of unscented cat box filler (with only a small amount of scented filler) into the depression and lower the toilet seat, while keeping the toilet seat cover up. Without the toilet seat down, the diameter of the porcelain rim will be too great and the balancing area too small. Now open the bathroom door and keep it open.

For cats following the Standard Method, the next visit to the bathroom will be a pivotal experience. Using position and smell as his guide, he will jump up onto the toilet seat and discover that the litter will not support him as securely as before. Therefore, he will circle round and round, eventually using the litter while balancing himself on the toilet seat.

Watch him to make certain this happens the *first* time he uses the new arrangement. Assuming that your cat is reasonably intelligent, he will analyze the situation and position himself over the litter, balanced on the edge of the toilet seat, right away. If not, you must confine him to the bathroom until he gets the idea. Once he learns to perform properly, the combination of jumping, expressing himself while balancing, and the resulting pleasure will form the complete "chain" that allows the cat to remember his new behavior.

For cats following the Alternate Method, simply watch and be patient. Because you've taken extra time and allowed the cat to perfect his balance on the spare toilet seat, the sudden absence of a litter box will not throw him off using the toilet.

DAY

18

Replace the plastic stretched across the porcelain rim with a new sheet after each usage. Yet this time, cut a two-inch-diameter hole in the center of the plastic. Attach the plastic as before, sprinkling litter *around* the hole, leaving the hole itself exposed. At this point, the cat will jump up, balance himself on the toilet seat as before, see the litter with the hole in the center, and do his business as though nothing had changed. This time, however, he will see and smell water, and hear a distinctly audible sound as he eliminates.

DAY

19

Now make a slightly larger hole in the plastic, three inches across, using even less litter than before. By now, the water beneath the plastic should be clearly visible—another link in the "chaining behavior" that tells the cat to jump up, balance, relieve himself into the now-diminished "litter," and jump down. Experienced in the ways of toiletry, your cat should feel quite secure on his new perch. The end of the tunnel is clearly in sight.

DAY

20

By this point, your cat should be completely adjusted to using the toilet, allowing you to dispense with the plastic wrap and cat litter. As long as you keep the toilet cover up, the seat down, and the bathroom door open, nothing will go awry.

DAY

21

Now, as you step away from the dark tunnel into the full light of day, take a moment to think of what you've accomplished. No more litter box, no more litter, no more cleaning and no more smell!

As a symbol of your emancipation, remove all traces of your horrible old litter-box life — the box itself, the excess litter, cleaning tools, as well as the plastic wrap and adhesive tape you used during the past few days. All contain traces of the smell that drives you and your cat mad. Besides, you will not need them any longer. While you're at it, clean the bathroom, removing any leftover smell of litter, keeping the bathroom door open and the toilet lid up (with the seat down).

Finally, give your cat a friendly pat on the head and yourself a well-deserved pat on the back.

5

MAINTAINING A LITTER-FREE CAT

O nce the training phase is completed and you settle into a new routine, maintaining your toilet trained cat will be simplicity itself, so long as you give him the same access to the bathroom as you did his litter box and periodic praise for a job well done.

DAILY MAINTENANCE

For households with more than one bathroom, it's wise to keep all bathroom doors ajar and toilet seats ready just in case your cat feels the urge. Even when trained using one bathroom, most cats eventually realize that all toilets are more or less the same. Given time, most cats will eventually claim every bathroom in the house. This even extends to using other people's toilets!

Yet not even the most desperate cat can pass through a closed bathroom door or lift a toilet cover that someone has left down. So to ensure complete access, it might be wise to post a sign in every bathroom as a reminder to family — and especially guests (baby sitters, neighbors, housekeepers, etc.) who might want to use the facilities — that they are sharing the house with a toilet-trained cat.

Remember, the most common reason for a cat's failing to use the toilet once he has been trained is because someone failed to leave the door open.

If you should leave the door open but accidentally leave the toilet cover down, don't be surprised if your cat jumps up on the next available porcelain-covered object — such as your bathtub or basin. Certainly, the cat's using the basin is preferable to his using the floor. But allowing him to do so more than occasionally is dangerous! Not only does it leave a telltale scent that might cause the cat to return to that spot, it diminishes the "chaining behavior" that you worked so hard to achieve.

OCCASIONAL SLIPUPS

Even the cleanest and best-trained cat will occasionally break training under certain circumstances. If this happens, try to track down the cause and correct the circumstance before it changes the cat's new behavior. Always look for the obvious first.

Physical reasons. Assuming that the cat has complete access to the toilet, the most frequent cause of changing behavior is physical. Obviously, no animal will perform as expected if he's physically ill. Most owners assume that if their cat is sick, they will detect it *before* the problem becomes serious. But this is not always the case.

The most widespread illness of this kind, Feline Urologic Syndrome (FUS), is difficult to spot in its early stages. Common among cats that eat commercial cat food with a high ash content, FUS begins as a bladder infection, cystitis, which mounts a silent assault on the cat's lower urinary tract, causing the urine to concentrate as it inflames the bladder. If left untreated, FUS causes mucus and other organic material to accumulate in the bladder, often resulting in urinary blockage, a painful condition that escalates with remarkable (and deadly) speed. Unable to urinate, the cat's kidneys shut down within hours, causing poisonous wastes to build up in the cat's bloodstream. Unless the blockage is swiftly removed by a veterinarian, FUS can result in severe internal damage and even death.

If caught in time, however, blockage needn't be fatal. Your cat will need expert medical care, as well as a change in diet. A dash of tomato juice in his food will help restore the acid in his blood that helps prevent infection. Once he has recovered, he will more than likely return to the toilet as though nothing had happened, with little or no retraining.

Psychological Reasons. If your cat fails to use the john once in a while and isn't physically ill, there's no reason to panic. Possibly he's just a little under the weather. More likely, the cat is upset or preoccupied about something and has lost his concentration — or is retaliating against something that is not to his liking.

Aside from refusing to eat, the most common sign of emotional distress in cats is stopping his normal housebroken behavior.

It's quite common for a cat to express his displeasure or distress by leaving a deposit in significant places: next to the new baby's crib, perhaps, or in the foyer of your new home. He may also deliberately defecate or urinate shortly after he has been disciplined as a way of showing his displeasure or defiance. If this happens, it's important to remain calm. When dealing with a cat, it's never wise to retaliate without considering your options. Quite often, an intentional slipup is nothing more than a momentary reaction, a sign of aggression that passes like a dark cloud. If so, your cat will quickly return to using the toilet, not only because he knows how to do it, but because he prefers it.

Remember that cats are very sensitive to their environment. The long absence (or death) of someone in the family, the birth of a baby, the acquisition or removal of another pet, or even the presence of a new boyfriend, girlfriend, or relative can add a layer of stress that causes some cats to go haywire for a day or two. Any sudden change in the household (such as a large, noisy party), sadness, or sudden trauma can cause a cat to stop using the toilet temporarily.

Yet by giving you this reaction, your cat might be asking for extra attention, privacy, or consolation. Should you suspect a psychological cause for a slipup, try to provide your cat with all the kind words and physical assurances that you can muster. While many cats become the center of attention when they first enter a household, sometimes the bloom leaves the rose after a year or two. If this should happen, your cat might be desperate for attention and unable to express it. This, plus emotional or territorial stress you're not even aware of, may cause him to seek attention in the only way he knows.

If misbehavior persists, remember these tips for preventing future "accidents":

1. Check with a vet to rule out bladder infections and any other physical ailments. Once detected, never wait for a physical problem to "pass in the night." Your cat may pass away instead.

2. Consider changing or improving your cat's environment. Get some new toys, a new scratching post, or, better still, clear some space that the cat can call his own. A moderately high bookshelf, four or five feet from the floor, for example, can be a comfortable place to rest while a cat watches his "territory." Any way that you can expand your cat's territory will help alleviate stress.

3. If the behavior persists, take the cat to the bathroom immediately after he eats, place a few drops of ammonia (which smells like urine) in the toilet, and, if necessary, confine him there until he performs properly.

4. Remove urine from the carpet or floor by using a commercial product such as Nature's Miracle, Nilodor, or plain white vinegar followed by club soda or seltzer to neutralize the odor. If he persists, place his food dish directly over the spot.

OLDER CATS

Even though cats undergo many of the same physical, chemical, and behavioral changes people do, many owners fail to notice that their cats are aging until they are truly "old." This is usually because old age does not affect a cat's behavior as radically as it does a human's. Unlike us, cats enjoy a prolonged middle age, eating as greedily at fifteen as they did when they were three. Properly exercised and fed, your cat's decline might be so gradual that you won't even notice until it is quite advanced.

Though it's impossible to estimate the life span of the "average" domestic cat, a general rule of thumb suggests that a healthy cat should live between fifteen and eighteen years and begin to suffer from genuine "old age" only after twelve or thirteen years. A rough comparison of equivalent ages would look something like this:

Felis catus	*Homo sapiens*
1 year	16 years
3 years	28 years
8 years	48 years
12 years	64 years
15 years	76 years
20 years	96 years

By the time he is fifteen, you will probably notice your cat spending longer periods asleep and perhaps taking less care of his grooming. But don't look for your aging cat to go gray in the way that most humans and dogs do. On the contrary, many cats do the opposite. For example, Siamese and Himalayan cats, whose dark markings (around the ears, nose, paws, and tail) depend on these parts of the body being at a lower temperature than the rest, frequently turn dark all over as poorer circulation lowers skin temperature as a whole.

The fact that older cats tend to feel the cold more than those in the prime of life is generally linked to reduced agility and increased indolence — all of which are part of the natural aging process.

But just because your cat is advancing to his brittle years doesn't mean he can't continue to practice his skills at the toilet. In fact, toilet-trained cats tend to stay younger and keep their jumping and balancing skills far longer than ordinary box-trained felines for the same reason that joggers enter old age with more spark in their step than sedentary adults.

Indeed many toilet-trained cats have been known to use the toilet without interruption well into their fifteenth or sixteenth year. Some become so set in their ways that they resent any change, which is ideal as far as toilet training is concerned. Eventually, however, even the most determined feline may need a little help. Usually, jumping is the first skill to diminish. Therefore, you might make the jump a little easier by arranging some steps next to the john.

Even if your cat can make the leap, he might prefer not to do so merely to answer the call of nature. He may also be less able to tolerate long periods without access to the bathroom. Should this become a real problem, it might be a kindness to reintroduce a litter box somewhere else in the home.

LIVING WITH AN OLDER TOILET-TRAINED CAT

Being aware of the changes that come with age can make a cat's final years both happier and healthier with just a little extra care. Remember, nothing ages a cat faster than stress. One of the principle benefits of toilet training is to remove the largest element of stress in a cat's life — his litter box — not to mention the various chemicals in commercial litter and parasites and diseases associated with the cat's own wastes, all of which affect the immune system, leaving him vulnerable to various opportunistic infections. But as the aging process takes its toll, physical and emotional stress can become the real problem, and, in extreme cases, can even deliver a death blow.

Situations that upset the older cat, such as long separations, should also be avoided if possible. Moving from one home to another, especially to a temporary home recently occupied by another cat, can be extremely traumatic for an older cat. To a 20-year-old cat, all alone in a strange place with the smell of another cat that he can neither see nor hear, such a shock can be debilitating, if not deadly.

EXTRA CARE

Once the cat passes the age of ten or twelve, high-quality, nourishing food becomes extremely important—as long as you don't overfeed him. Because they are more sedentary, older cats have a much lower metabolic rate than younger ones.

In old age, most mammals appear to "shrink"—naturally losing up to a third of their lean body tissue. Many cat owners see this shrinkage as a sign of hunger and feed their older cats more when they should be feeding them less. As a result, lean tissue is replaced by fat, producing another, more subtle but equally fatal, form of stress.

On the other hand, an aging cat may refuse food.

As they age, many cats lose their sense of smell. This is dangerous, because cats will generally not eat when they cannot smell. Thus, it is wise to occasionally stimulate the cat's nose by seasoning his food with a bit of strong fish, increased vitamin and mineral supplements, and an extra teaspoon of butter to maintain a healthy coat.

With each passing year, it becomes more difficult for a cat to groom himself for the half hour it takes to reach every spot on his body. Why not lighten his burden by a daily grooming? A simple brushing takes only minutes. Not only will it stimulate his coat, it will make him much more responsive. Nail clipping, as usual, should be done by your veterinarian.

Thus, with proper diet, love, and a little extra care, your cat's final years can (and should) be the best years of his life.

6

FREQUENTLY ASKED QUESTIONS

Don't cats have a compulsion to dig elsewhere when the litter box is removed?

This varies from one cat to the next. While some owners notice their cats pawing around the houseplants more than usual, others see no such reaction. According to researchers, the feline compulsion to dig loose dirt is an autonomic response associated with the smell of urine and feces. The reaction is literally "hardwired" into their brain. Indeed, the same response is triggered by the smell of certain foods. Remove the smell and you also remove the desire to dig.

How do I know my cat is the right age to be toilet trained?

Any cat between the age of six months and ten or eleven years can be toilet trained. Generally, the younger they are, the more quickly they learn. So don't make the mistake of putting off training until the cat is more "mature." At six months of age, your cat is equipped with all of the brainpower he's ever likely to have. But if your cat is past his prime, don't despair. Old habits may die hard, but they do pass eventually. With a little extra time and practice, even the most stubborn old cat will come around.

Doesn't the sound of rushing water make a cat uneasy?

Hardly. Compared to their ancestors, who lived for millions of years in north Africa and the Middle East, where oases are few and far between, modern cats love the sight and sound of water. Stories about the cat's love of water abound. For example, the author Carl Van Vechten had a celebrated Persian named Ariel who enjoyed jumping into the bathtub, head-first, every time someone took a bath. Certain breeds, such as the

Turkish Vann — known for its fluffy white coat, large paws, and busy amber tail — not only swim, but actually *fish* for their dinner using their paws and teeth.

Can a cat learn to flush the toilet when he's finished?

Don't count on it. Unlike *using* the toilet, flushing does not involve any of the cat's standard paw or body movements. Besides, the average toilet requires more pressure on the lever than the average cat can muster. So, unless you intend to buy a modern, touch-sensitive electronic toilet any time soon, plan on flushing the john yourself.

How does pregnancy affect a toilet trained cat?

It is common for a pregnant female to stop using the toilet from the time she begins to "show" (approximately midway into her pregnancy) until the time her kittens are fully weaned and on their own. Not only is it easier for her to use the box when she's pregnant, she will *need* the box to teach her kittens the ancient skills of digging and burying that all kittens need to learn. Therefore, *it is essential that you make a litter box available as soon as you realize that your cat is pregnant*, giving her ample time to decide when she should begin using it again.

Just as in humans, pregnancy in cats sets off a

chain reaction that changes the mother's "normal" behavior pattern. Though the details of this process are not fully understood, pregnancy seems to unlock an ancient memory within the mother's brain, causing her to behave in ways that resemble mothers in the wild. From the moment she delivers her kittens, many of her actions — such as nursing, cleaning her kittens, moving the nest, and dragging "prey" to them, even when it comes from a can — are consistent with the ancient patterns that all cats follow, both in human homes and in the wild.

Can I retrain a mother *with* her kittens?

As long as the mother was toilet trained prior to her pregnancy, training her kittens with her will be easier than training the kittens on their own. Deciding how soon to introduce toilet training will depend on how many kittens you decide to keep. Rather than train kittens that you plan to give away, wait until all "extra" kittens are gone before reintroducing the 21-Day Program.

During the fifth or sixth month, you can begin to raise the box *slowly*, making sure that the kittens follow their mother's lead. (Since training is nothing new to the mother, she should take to the program immediately.) By watching their mother, the kittens will follow her every action — assuming they are large enough to jump the full fourteen inches to reach the toilet seat. Should you sense any resistance as you eliminate the litter in the final phase, proceed slowly.

Can a cat that goes outdoors also be toilet trained?

Both wild cats and free-ranging domestics define their territory using their scent glands and wastes as markers. Thus, every time your cat ventures outdoors, he explores and marks new areas by face rubbing, clawing, and later by urinating and defecating. In this way, the cat's territory gradually expands until it encompasses not only your own backyard, but your neighbors' as well (assuming they do not have any cats or dogs). Once established, the cat maintains this territory by leaving his wastes in a variety of places, forming a pattern not unlike the scent barrier that feral cats use to protect and orient themselves in the wild.

Cats that venture out on a regular schedule tend to use their litter boxes less (often much less) than they would if they were confined indoors. Therefore, unless you live in a climate that keeps your cat indoors for long periods of time (such as the Pacific Northwest, where it can rain for days or weeks at a time, or Minnesota, where winter lasts up to eight months a year), he will probably prefer to go outdoors rather than stay inside and use a litter box.

Generally speaking, a cat that does not use a litter box regularly will not take to toilet training. Yet there are exceptions (see "The Cat Who Trained Himself," p. 27). Therefore, cats that move from the country to the city will accept toilet training only after they have been thoroughly litter trained.

What are the chances of "catching something" from my toilet-trained cat?

Whether toilet trained or not, any cat that goes outdoors or spends time with infected cats or dogs (or humans) can catch fleas, parasites or ringworm. In general, however, these ailments are much more easily transmitted via bedclothes, furniture, and carpeting. Since transmittal is via the cat's fur, and not his paws, the likelihood of "catching something" from your toilet seat is extremely low.

HOW DO I TALK TO MY CAT?

Most people do not realize the effect they have on their pet every time they open their mouths," says Brian Kilcommons, a pet training consultant at the Tufts School of Veterinary Medicine and president of The Family Dog, Inc.,

How Do Cats Talk to Each Other?

E veryone knows that cats make noises when they are happy, sad, confused, frightened, or angry. The variety and complexity of feline vocalization has been a popular topic among specialists. Decoding these messages, however, has not progressed beyond isolating the most obvious feline messages. Here are a few:

Murmur patterns

Purr ['hrn-rhn-'hrn-rhn ...]

Greeting (request) ['mhrn]

Call ['e mhrn]

Acknowledgment ['mhrn-n']

Vowel patterns

Demand ['mhrn-a':ou]

Begging demand ['mhrn-a:ou]

Bewilderment ['maou:?]

Whisper ['mhrn-E']

Complaint ['mhn-a:ou]

Anger [wa:ou:]

Distress patterns

Growl [grrr ...]

Hiss ['sss ...]

Refusal [æ*'æ'æ']

Snarl ['æ:o]

Scream [æ!]

Mating cry ['ø-ø:e]

Pronunciation:

[a] as in father

[æ] as in cat

[E] as in get

[e] as in momma

[o] as in go

[ø] as in the French eux

[n] as in sung

[u] as in pool

[:] indicates prolongation

['] indicates stress accent

['] indicates inhalation

[*] indicates wavering

in New York. Of course, cats do not understand English (or any language except their own). Nonetheless, each time you speak, your pet quickly registers the tone of your voice and responds accordingly. "For this reason," adds Kilcommons, "it's important to use your voice properly when toilet training your cat."

To this end, Kilcommons suggests that owners try to master three different ways of speaking, each with its own intonation and function:

Your upper register should be reserved for praise, delivered with enthusiasm, the kinder and more heartfelt the better. Whenever your cat does something well, give him a verbal pat on the back ("Good kitten!") by raising the *tone* of your voice, without lapsing into baby talk. "The higher your intonation, the more your cat will respond," says Kilcommons, "assuming that you don't go overboard." Try to make eye contact when praising your cat. This way, when he hears your voice, your cat will look up.

Your normal or middle register should be reserved for commands. Try to limit the number of commands to a handful of words — such as "Come," "Down," and "Stop" — making each command as short and distinct as possible. Be emphatic. "When giving a command," says Kilcommons, "you're not negotiating or pleading with the cat, you're *telling* him what you want in a direct, non-threatening manner." This way, you eventually teach the cat to respond to the sound of your voice. "If you give a command and the cat does not respond, be prepared to enforce your instruction *gently*," he adds, "then praise him warmly using your higher intonation, offering a gentle stroke to help reinforce the new behavior. That way, you give the cat incentive to respond the next time."

Your lower register should be reserved only for extreme displeasure. Remember, there's no need to yell to get your message across. Simply lower your voice, say "Stop it," then praise him when he responds.

Delivered with the proper conviction, followed by immediate corrective action (but no hitting *ever*), the words "Stop it" have a magical effect on most cats. "The sound is both sharp and distinct," says Kilcommons. "This makes it easy to recognize amid the blizzard of talk that most cats prefer to ignore." Yet it's important not to overuse "Stop it," particularly when toilet training. After all, when a cat in training does something that is almost (but not quite) correct, saying "Stop it" may cause him to stop training altogether.

Another tip: "Don't repeat a command over and over, hoping for a response," says Kilcommons. "Instead, use clear, one-word commands with your middle tone, enforce the command *firmly but gently* if needed, then praise with your higher tone, followed by a gentle stroke." In general, you should praise a cat more than you correct.

BIBLIOGRAPHY

Beaver, B. "Feline Behavioral Problems," *Veterinary Clinician of North America,* volume 6, August 1976, pp. 333–340.

————, *Veterinary Aspects of Feline Behavior.* St. Louis: C. V. Mosby, 1980.

Camuti, L. J. *All My Patients Are Under the Bed, Memoirs of a Cat Doctor.* New York: Simon and Schuster 1980.

Chesler, P. "Maternal Influence in Learning by Observation in Kittens," *Science,* volume 166, 1969, pp. 901–902.

Ewer, R. F. "Further Observations on Suckling Behavior in Kittens, Together with Some General Considerations of Interrelations of Innate and Acquired Responses," *Behavior,* volume 17, 1961, pp. 247–260.

Fox, M. *Understanding Your Cat.* New York: Bantam, 1977.

Gurney, E. *How to Live with a Calculating Cat.* Englewood Cliffs: Prentice-Hall, 1962.

Hart, B. V. "Learning Ability in Cats," *Journal of Feline Practice,* September/October, 1975.

Jones, E. and B. J. Coman. "Ecology of the feral cat, *Felis catus,*" *Australian Wildlife Research,* volume 9, 1982, pp. 409–420.

Kerr, M. *An Introduction to Cat Care.* New York: Chartwell Books, 1988.

Kling, A., J. K. Kovach, and T. J. Tucker. "The Behavior of Cats," *The Behavior of Domestic Animals,* edited by E. S. Hafez, Baltimore: Williams & Williams, Co., 1969.

Kuo, Z. Y. "The genesis of the cat's response to the rat," *Journal of Comparative Psychology,* volume 11, 1930, pp. 1–35.

Leyhausen, P. *Cat Behavior: the Predatory and Social Behavior of Domestic and Wild Cats.* New York: Garland Publishing, 1979.

Macdonald, Apps, Carr, and Kerby. "Social Dynamics, Nursing Coalitions . . . Among Farm Cats," *Felis catus, Advances in Ethology,* 1987, volume 28, pp. 1–64.

Morris, D. *Catwatching.* New York: Crown, 1986.

————— , *Catlore.* New York: Crown, 1987.

Moser, P. W. "Are Cats Smart? Yes, At Being Cats," *Discover,* May 1987, pp. 77–84.

————— , "Filler's the Name, Odor's the Game," *Fortune Magazine,* April 25, 1988, pp. 107–115.

Panaman, R. "Behavior and Ecology of Free-Ranging Female Farm Cats *(Felis catus),"* in *Zeitschrift für Tierpsychologie,* volume 56, 1981, pp. 59–73;

Rosenblatt, J. S. "Learning in Newborn Kittens," *Scientific American,* volume 227, 1972, pp. 18–25.

Rule, P. M. *The Cat, with an essay on feline instinct.* London: S. Sonnenschein, Lowray and Co., 1887.

Taylor, D. *You and Your Cat.* New York: Knopf, 1986.

Thorpe, W. H. *Learning and Instinct in Animals.* Boston: Harvard University Press, 1963.

Turner, D. C. and P. Bateson. *The Domestic Cat, the biology of its behavior.* London: Cambridge University Press, 1988.

Van Vechten, C. *A Tiger in the House.* New York: Knopf, 1920.

Verberne, G. and P. Leyhausen. "Marking behavior of some *Viverridae* and *Felidae:* time-interval analysis of pattern marking," *Behavior,* volume 58, 1976, pp. 192–253.

Warren, J. M. and A. Baron. "The Formation of Learning Sets by Cats," *Journal of Comparative Physiology,* volume 49, June 1956, pp. 227–231.